"What defies for ordinary people understanding, is the truth that one man could carry in the totality of that design, could somehow construe from the first note to the last, a coherent immensity of a complexity which defied analysis."

- George Steiner, University of Cambridge

Opera Journeys™ *Mini Guide Series*

Opera Classics Library™ *Series*

Opera Journeys™ *Libretto Series*
A History of Opera:
Milestones and Metamorphoses

Mozart's Da Ponte Operas

PUCCINI COMPANION

Verdi Companion: 27 Opera Study Guide

WWW.OPERAJOURNEYS.COM

Richard Wagner

The Ring of the Nibelung

("Der Ring des Nibelungen")

OPERA CLASSICS LIBRARY™ SERIES

Edited by Burton D. Fisher
Principal lecturer, *Opera Journeys Lecture Series*

Opera Journeys™ Publishing / Boca Raton, Florida

WEB SITE: www.operajourneys.com   E MAIL: operaj@bellsouth.net

Contents

(continued)

a *prelude....*

OPERA CLASSICS LIBRARY

The Ring of the Nibelung

Richard Wagner's *The Ring of the Nibelung* is a colossus of music theater, a powerful music drama that absorbs its listeners into profound universal themes and ideas that are primal and timeless; in all respects, the *Ring* addresses the political, philosophical and cultural values of the nineteenth-century Western world.

The *Inspirations for the Ring of the Nibelung* commentary in this text evolves from Wagner's own writings during his revolutionary period: "I will destroy the existing order of things. So up, you people of the earth! Up, you mourners, you oppressed, you poor!" Wagner had become outraged by his contemporary society's inequities, injustices and evils. The *Ring* represented his philosophical solution for the world's ills, a vision in which the world of evil would become redeemed through love.

Each of the four music dramas in *The Ring of the Nibelung* is presented in this text with appropriate background and synopsis, its *Principal Characters,* and a comprehensive *Story Narrative with Music Highlight Examples;* the latter includes over 90 original music transcriptions of themes and leitmotifs that are interspersed within the story's dramatic exposition. In addition, the text includes a*Dictionary of Opera and Musical Terms.*

As Wagner boldly theorized in his "Gesamtkunstwerk" ("the total artwork"), the opera art form is the sum of many artistic expressions: theatrical drama, music, scenery, poetry, dance, acting and gesture. In opera, it is the composer who is the dramatist, using the emotive power of his music to express intense human conflicts. Words evoke thought, but music provokes feelings; opera's sublime fusion of words and music is integrated with all the theatrical arts and provides powerful theater, an impact on one's sensibilities that can reach into the very depths of the human soul.

Wagner's *The Ring of the Nibelung* is certainly a "Gesamtkunstwerk": a glorious operatic invention that represents a tribute to the art form as well as to its ingenious composer.

Burton D. Fisher
Editor
OPERA CLASSICS LIBRARY

The Ring of the Nibelung

("Der Ring des Nibelungen")

Music composed by Richard Wagner

Dramas written by Richard Wagner

———————

The Rhinegold ("Das Rheingold")
Premiere in 1869 at the Hoftheater, Munich

The Valkyrie ("Die Walküre")
Premiere in 1870 at the Hoftheater, Munich

Siegfried
Premiere in 1876 at Bayreuth

Twilight of the Gods ("Götterdämmerung")
Premiere in 1876 at Bayreuth

———————

Inspirations for The Ring of the Nibelung

Wagner's ancient mythological sources for his music-drama colossus, *The Ring of the Nibelung*, portrayed a turbulent world in which sinister and evil forces unconscionably lusted for power. He adapted the basic universal themes of those myths to create an allegory to deconstruct the moral values of his nineteenth-century century contemporary world: the *Ring*'s underlying conflicts and tensions expressed Wagner's moral outrage at the decadence and degeneration of his society's philosophical, political, social and economic values.

Wagner, like most contemporary nineteenth-century visionaries, considered himself a child of the previous century's Enlightenment, the heir to hopes and dreams that social progress and the ideals of human dignity would transform the evils and injustices of society. But the dream was shattered in the malaise following the French Revolution, when the restored authoritarian rulers of post-Napoleonic Europe became involved in a fiercely competitive struggle for political and economic power, heedless and reluctant to institute social reforms.

The Industrial Revolution had transformed society through its rapid changes in methods and mechanization; there was a new focus on machine rather than land. And in that transition new classes of society emerged. The bourgeoisie and middle classes became the new claimants to the old legitimacy, and a large class of working poor who were ignorant and illiterate, clamored for social progress. The old order of inherited title and property became involved in a battle for power against new forces that benefited from the industrial-capitalist system. A greater disparity arose between wealth and poverty, provoking deeper divisions to emerge in the social order. By the mid-nineteenth century, European society seemed to have become more profoundly divided by political, social, and economic realities; it was a division that created new claims to power, and ever more dramatically separated the dominators from the dominated, and the wealthy from the poor.

As Wagner viewed his contemporary society, he became a cultural pessimist, perceiving his world as decadent, immoral and unjust, a degeneration that was the result of an obsessive lust for material wealth and power that he considered the root of all evil. The *Ring of the Nibelung* became Wagner's *cri de coeur,* his impassioned artistic expression of disdain and condemnation of society's vices and follies. In his saga, the protagonists — Gods, Giants and Dwarfs — are allegorically the decadent immoral forces of his contemporary society: the politicians, the authoritarian church, and the bourgeoisie, et al.

From inspiration to fulfillment, *The Ring of the Nibelung* engaged Wagner for 26 years. During that long evolutionary period, his impassioned social critique became more profound and visionary as he became absorbed in the philosophical ideas of Ludwig Feuerbach and Arthur Schopenhauer. In *Twilight of the Gods*, the old order of Gods is destroyed in a cataclysm, what Wagner considered a necessary retribution for their despicable evil and the forced imposition of their Will. But Wagner concluded the *Ring* saga with a profound sense of hope, a sense of optimism in which the world had been redeemed and purified from its Curse of evil, and that a new sense of humanity would arise to inspire humanity toward a new moral order of lofty ideals and elevated conscience.

The Enlightenment awakened the soul of Europe to renewed optimism. It nurtured the hope that democratic progress would consolidate egalitarian ideals, and that economically, the industrialization of Europe would decrease the disparity between wealth and poverty.

The Enlightenment inspired the French Revolution. Napoleon arose from its ashes, his primary crusade to destroy those traditional enemies of human dignity and freedom, the oppressive autocratic and tyrannical European monarchies, in particular, the Austrian Hapsburg Empire. (That goal was finally achieved one hundred years later at the conclusion of World War I.)

Wagner was born in Leipzig in 1813 amid the clamor and devastation of the "Battle of the Nations," Napoleon's defeat by the victorious Grand Alliance: the coalition of England, Russia, Prussia and Austria. After their victory, the European powers sought revenge against the liberal and democratic ideals fomented by the French Revolution, ultimately exercising severe military force not only to quell discontent, but also to consolidate their power.

Napoleon and France had threatened the social order of Europe and upset its delicate political power balances. In the aftermath of Napoleon, the victors strove to consolidate and strengthen their national power; the Hohenzollern King of Prussia, Frederick William III, acquired the Kingdom of Saxony, an attempt to strengthen Prussian power in order to offset the traditional dominance of Austria in German affairs, a reward that was justified by the treacherous collaboration of Saxony's King Frederick Augustus I with Napoleon; the Austrian Hapsburgs, badly weakened by Napoleon, were prompted by Prince Klemens von Metternich to create a newly strengthened France that would balance Austrian fears of Russian opportunism.

In 1815, after Napoleon's defeat, the Congress of Vienna attempted to stabilize Europe's balance of power by imposing a peace settlement with France that preserved it as a great European power, conceding to reduce it to its ancient rather than natural borders. They reorganized the German Confederation by consolidating its original 300 states into 39 sovereign states, ostensibly providing it with a renewed strength that would represent a barrier against any future expansion by France into the Rhineland. With the balance of power established, the Congress of Vienna created a bulwark of powerful states to thwart fears of possible future expansion of the Russian colossus into Western Europe, as well as deter the reemergence of a threatening France.

But the ultimate reality of the Congress of Vienna was that the Quadruple Alliance of Austria, Prussia, Great Britain, and Russia, had essentially imposed themselves as the unwanted guardians over most of the European states; they had become rulers of nations who were heedless to national cultural or ethnic sympathies and inclinations. As such, many nations were ruled by foreign powers: Greece, Czechoslovakia, Holland, Belgium, Poland, Hungary, Italy, and particularly, the German Confederation of States. During the 1840s, Wagner lived in Dresden, Saxony, a state in the German Confederation that was politically allied with Prussia.

The Post-Napoleonic restoration of unwanted foreign rule and its inherent oppression and tyranny, provoked the growth of romantic dreams of nationhood and self-determination, the idea that being kin, numerous, and strong was a means toward achieving social and political stability and progress.

The French Revolution had awakened dreams of human progress, and those dreams failed to be suppressed by Napoleon's defeat. There was an impassioned clamor for social and political reform, the abolition of poverty, and the inauguration of economic freedoms. The ruling European monarchies promised social and democratic reforms but failed to provide them. Ultimately, frustration, anxiety, and an uneasy political equilibrium exploded into social unrest and revolutionary riots in virtually every major city in Europe. During the years 1815 to 1848, there were armed revolts by liberals, democrats and socialists, which were countered with fierce and oppressive repression by the ruling authoritarian powers.

The uprisings were twofold in purpose: firstly, they demanded social and political reform; and secondly, they represented outcries for national identity, self-determination, and liberation from alien rule. Similarly, Wagner had become consumed by German nationalism, the idea of uniting the various German states into one federation. Nevertheless, the monarchies remained the unwanted custodians of nations, and were unhesitant to invite neighboring allied armies to intervene and quell domestic uprisings: the "Metternich System" that was created by the Congress of Vienna.

In Saxony, where the thirty-five year old Richard Wagner was kapellmeister (orchestra director) at the Dresden Court Opera, social unrest and nationalist fervor exploded in 1848-1849. An uprising was sparked by the political actions of the harsh, oppressive, indignant, and tyrannical "foreign" ruler of Saxony, the Prussian king, Friedrich Wilhelm IV. Aside from their social and political frustrations, the Saxons became exasperated after the Prussians, fearful and paranoid about threats from the east, appeased the Russian Czar with a peace treaty, a détente that the Saxons interpreted as an utter betrayal.

Wagner was obsessed by his utopian dreams for social and political progress. At the time he wrote: "In 1848 the fight for Man against existing society began...the determination of Man is to achieve, through ever greater perfecting of his spiritual, moral and physical powers, a higher, purer happiness."

Wagner viewed the landscape of possible progress and became disappointed, disillusioned, skeptical and despairing. Ultimately he vented his discontent by becoming an active and impetuous revolutionary, what was deemed an anarchist in his times, but a terrorist in contemporary times.

Wagner perceived the existing political powers as corrupt and abusive; he condemned nouveau riche materialism as the cause of the degeneration of society's values. And at the Dresden State Opera, he became frustrated by the pettiness of the politically appointed opera management, who refused to produce his newest opera, *Lohengrin,* perhaps their censorship because the opera story strongly ennobled German nationalism through the characterization of King Henry the Fowler, the exalted historic king of Saxony.

Wagner was also embittered by his personal failures; he was broke, debt-ridden, and frequently fled to other cities to escape creditors. The solution and panacea to his frustrations was to actively advocate socialist ideology; in the process he became a violent anticapitalist, and an audacious socialist and communist who advocated the abolition of capital. (Marx, born in 1818, five years after Wagner, published his Manifesto in 1848.) Wagner, now a rabid revolutionary, joined radical groups like the Hegelians, who protested religious and intellectual values. At the same time, he befriended the notorious Russian anarchist, Mikhail Bakunin, who incited him to terrorism: Wagner manufactured and distributed grenades, and wrote anonymous newspaper articles and inflammatory political tracts that endorsed armed insurrection and revolt against the prevailing powers.

All of Wagner's personal anxieties, revolutionary ideology, German nationalism, and anti-Prussianism, suddenly materialized into action, and he became inspired to actively participate in the 1848 Dresden uprising against the government. The revolt led to bloodshed after Prussian troops were summoned by the Saxon King to quell the rebellion. In the aftermath, Wagner was banished from Germany, forced to flee to Zurich where he began twelve long years of exile, defeated, disheartened and shattered by the failure of his utopian social dreams.

But perhaps the final blow to his dreams for social progress occurred while he was in exile in Zurich. In December 1851, Louis Napoleon, nephew of Napoleon Bonaparte and son of Napoleon's brother, transformed France's pseudo-democracy into a dictatorship, capitalizing on most Frenchmen's desire to restore order after their own disturbances of 1848. After Napoleon was elected President of France, he eloquently expounded the ideals of liberty, swore to uphold the constitution, and ingeniously created the illusion that the masses participated in his government through universal suffrage. Nevertheless, from the outset, Napoleon planned to overthrow the Republic and create a new empire. With one stroke of Napoleon's pen, France's Second Republic was transformed into a presidential dictatorship in which Napoleon was granted full powers to institute martial law and dominate legislative matters; Prince Louis Napoleon became Napoleon III, the totalitarian dictator of France's Second Empire.

As Wagner read about Louis Napoleon's coup d'etat, his optimism of 1848 transformed more profoundly into resignation and despair. The restoration of Empire in France made him even more skeptical and pessimistic about future social and political progress, and he concluded that society and its political institutions were unconscionably evil, unjust, and beyond salvation. The exiled ex-revolutionary firebrand of Dresden became consumed to voice his moral outrage and protest: his cri de coeur would be an impassioned artistic gospel that would portray the political and social horrors of his contemporary society: the music drama, *The Ring of the Nibelung.*

In 1849, six months after writing the first prose sketch for the *Ring*, Wagner wrote an iconoclastic prognosis for Europe's authoritarian societies: "I will destroy the domination of one over others. I will break down the power of the mighty, of the law, and of property. Let the madness be destroyed which gives one man power over millions, and subjects millions to the power of one man..."

The Ring of the Nibelung became Wagner's allegorical dramatization of human evil, immorality, and injustice, a work whose underlying essence he would endow with the philosophical profundity of Goethe and Shakespeare.

Wagner's pessimism and skepticism were synonymous with the ideology of the Romantic movement in art, literature, and music, a period that coincides chronologically with the political and social turmoil that began with the storming of the Bastille and the outbreak of the French Revolution in 1789, to the last urban uprisings that overcame almost every major European city in 1848.

Romanticism represented a pessimistic backlash against the optimism of the eighteenth-century Enlightenment and the Age of Reason; Rousseau, a spokesman of

Enlightenment ideals, had projected a new world of freedom and civility. But the Romanticists viewed those Enlightenment ideals of egalitarian progress as a mirage and illusion, elevated hopes and dreams that dissolved in the Reign of Terror (1892-94); that despair was reinforced by Napoleon's preposterous despotism, the post-Napoleonic return to autocratic tyranny and oppression, and the economic and social injustices nurtured by the Industrial Revolution.

The Reign of Terror and the subsequent devastation of the Napoleonic wars totally destroyed any dreams remaining from the Enlightenment. Like the Holocaust in the 20th century, those bloodbaths shook the very foundations of humanity by invoking man's deliberate betrayal of his highest nature and ideals; Schiller was prompted to reverse the idealism of his exultant "Ode to Joy" (1785) by concluding that the new century had "begun with murder's cry." To those pessimists — the Romanticists — the drama of human history was approaching doomsday, and civilization was on the verge of vanishing completely. Others concluded that the French Revolution and the Reign of Terror had ushered in a terrible new era of unselfish crimes in which men committed horrible atrocities out of love not of evil but of virtue. Like Goethe's Faust, who represented "two souls in one breast," man was considered a paradox, simultaneously the possessor of great virtue and wretched evil.

Romanticists sought alternatives to what had become their failed notions of human progress, and sought a panacea to their loss of confidence in the present as well as the future. As such, Romanticists developed a growing nostalgia for the past by seeking exalted histories that served to recall vanished glories: writers such as Sir Walter Scott, Alexandre Dumas, and Victor Hugo, penned tributes to past values of heroism and virtue that seemed to have vanished in their contemporary times. Intellectual and moral values had declined, and modern civilization was perceived as transformed into a society of philistines in which the ideals of refinement and polished manners had surrendered to a form of sinister decadence. Those in power were considered deficient in maintaining order, and instead of resisting the impending collapse of civilization and social degeneration, they were deemed to have embraced them feebly and without vigor.

Romanticists became preoccupied with the conflict between nature and human nature. Industrialization and modern commerce were considered the despoilers of the natural world: steam engines and smokestacks were viewed as dark manifestations of commerce and veritable images from hell. But natural man, uncorrupted by commercialism, was ennobled. So Romanticism sought escapes from society's horrible realities by appealing to strong emotions, the bizarre and the irrational, the instincts of self-gratification, and the search for pleasure and sensual delights.

Romanticists were seeking an alternative to the Christian path to salvation. The philosopher Immanuel Kant (1724-1804) strongly influenced early German Romanticism when he scrutinized the relationship between God and man, ultimately concluding that man — not God — was the center of the universe. Following Kant, David Friedrich Strauss wrote the extremely popular "Life of Christ" that deconstructed the Gospel. And finally, Nietzsche pronounced the death of God. Theologically and philosophically, German Romantics believed in the existence of God, but they were not turning to Christianity's Heaven for salvation and redemption, but rather, to the spiritual bliss provided by human love.

Ultimately, Romanticism's ideology posed the antithesis of material values by striving to raise consciousness to more profound emotions and aesthetic sensibilities; for the Romanticists, the spiritual path to God and human salvation could only be achieved through idealized human love and freedom, and Wagner's *The Ring of the Nibelung* faithfully expresses that Romanticist ideology to the core; its entire underlying essence emphasizes human salvation through love and compassion.

During Wagner's revolutionary period he became influenced by the philosophy of Ludwig Feuerbach (1804-72) to whom he dedicated "The Art-Work of the Future" (1849). Feuerbach articulated his iconoclastic theories in "Das Wesen des Christenthums," in which he deemed all religions — including Christianity — as mythical inventions, creations of a nonexistent God who was manifested through imaginary projections, or an idealization of the collective unconscious. As such, the supposed divine fallibility of church and state was deemed pure illusion, a tyrannical authority that had no claim for its existence, and was ripe for destruction and replacement by a new social order that was based firmly on the principles of human love and justice. Karl Marx hailed Feuerbach as the unwitting prophet of the social revolution he prophesied.

Wagner embraced Feuerbach's anticlericalism, firmly believing that church and state authority had an inherent unnaturalness and inhumanity that conditioned man away from his natural human instincts of creativity: man's primary needs of nature and love became compelling themes of the *Ring*. During the Enlightenment, Rousseau wrote: "Man was born free, and everywhere he is in chains," a conception that nurtured the ideal of the "noble savage," an implication that natural man possessed virtues that were uncorrupted by the evils of civilization. Wagner reasoned that man's instinctive need for love and fellowship explained its creation of myths, religion and art. And if the great myths were projections of humanity's highest ideals and aspirations, then religion served to impede man's natural inclinations by imposing an arbitrary system of rigid dogmas that supported the state rather than man. Wagner's ultimate conclusion was that the enemy of man was the authoritarian state and the church that opposed man's natural instincts, and particularly his freedom to love.

In "Civilization and its Discontents," Freud later postulated that there was a perpetual conflict between humanity's instincts for life – and love – that were being opposed and destroyed by man's aggressive and self-destructive instincts: authoritarian state power was considered a by-product of that aggression. As such, in man's struggle for survival, the weak ceded to the aggression of the strong, which served to repudiate humanity's nobler aspirations. In aggression-bred authoritarianism man became exploited, subjected by the strong, and abused by a privileged few who imposed their will on the many. Freud concluded that it was considered natural for instinctive man to live in a free society, and unnatural for man to live in a law-conditioned authoritarian state. Therefore, the state's rule became a crime against human nature, and therefore against nature itself.

Feuerbach's denunciation of the tyrannical church and state authoritarianism, combined with the idea of man's natural instincts for love and freedom, are themes expressed profoundly in all of the conflicts and tension of Wagner's *Ring*; if anything, those conflicts represent the core of the saga, the collision of forces that interfere with man's instinctive desire for love and freedom.

Essentially, Romanticists yearned for a world of idealized spiritualism that would replace mundane values. In Germany, in particular, those desires were manifested in "volkish" ("of the people") ideology, a prideful form of cultural nationalism that ennobled the intrinsic spirit of its people.

Germans specifically worried that industrialization would displace the cultural core of their society: farmers, artisans, and peasants. They believed that their people possessed the noble "volksseele" ("folk's soul"), a specific national ethos that was shared by kindred Germans and united them through their customs, arts, crafts, legends, traditions, and superstitions, values and virtues that had been passed on to them from generation to generation.

In the anthropological sense, Germans believed they possessed a unique — if not superior — "Kultur" (culture) that represented lofty spiritual achievements in art, literature, and history. As such, their "volk" (folk) heritage made them different from the rest of Europe in terms of their identity, communal purpose, and organic solidarity. Early German Romantics, such as J. G. Herder (1744-1803), the author of "Ideas on the Philosophy of History and Mankind" (1784), proposed that the "volk" had produced a living culture, which, despite its humble beginnings among peasants and artisans, represented the seedbed of the unique German Kultur; it was an exalted personality that was portrayed in their art, poetry, epic, music, and myth. As such, German culture was individual and different, and possessed its own particular "volksgeist" ("folk spirit") and "volksseele" ("folk's soul.")

The German conception of their Kultur was synonymous with their cultural nationalism. It represented the antithesis of Zivilization (civilization), a French perception of politeness and sophistication, urban society, materialism, commerce and superficiality. German Romantics were seeking a cultural renaissance, and yearning for independence from their perceived slavish adherence to alien intellectual and cultural standards: in particular, French cultural values and the "philosophes," which imposed literary and artistic values that contradicted the essence of their culture.

Although Germans were divided politically into separate states, they were united by language and culture. Romanticist Germans, like Wagner, opposed French Zivilization and urged Germans to return to their cultural past and awaken their powerful mythology that chronicled their roots and represented their vast spiritual history. Schiller aptly evoked the spirit of the German cultural renaissance: "Schöne Welt, wo bist du?" ("Beautiful world, where are you?") During this raising of their historical and cultural consciousness, writers, artists, philosophers and musicians revived neglected German ancient literature, sagas, legends, ballads, and fairy tales. They believed that this vast heritage of their "folk soul" possessed virtues of naturalness, a depth of knowledge, and spiritual human values that they deemed more profound than those existing in the surrounding world.

The most notable nineteenth-century excavators of the German past were the Grimm brothers, who energetically recovered myths and legends of the ancient German and Teutonic peoples. Through them, the twelfth-century Nibelungenlied was first translated into modern German, a spiritual epic, or German Iliad, that Romanticists believed captured the soul of German culture.

Wagner, like many of his contemporary intellectuals, considered the Nibelungenlied saga's central theme about the curse of gold synonymous with contemporary Europe's power-madness and materialism; the Nibelungenlied ultimately became the primary literary foundation for Wagner's epic *Ring*. And Wagner believed that his music dramas would revive the spirit of German culture; he actually envisioned that Goethe's *Faust*, up to that time their esteemed national poem, would yield its exalted place to his *Ring*.

German Romanticists and national culturists envisioned a national theater like that of the ancient Greeks that would dramatize their spiritual and mythic heritage. Greek theater was a form of ancient opera in which the drama was underscored with the emotive power of music. Thus, Wagner considered that his music dramas would become embraced as a national art form that would recapture the lofty humanistic aspirations of Greek tragedy. The music dramas would be ritually performed in a national opera that would become a consecrated temple of German art, a theater that would preserve the glories of their cultural heritage, elevate spiritual values, and 1 redeem those who erred. Through the greatness and profundity of the universal themes of Teutonic myth, Wagner intended to restore greatness to the German spirit and soul. With his epic *Ring* ritually performed at Bayreuth, he would recapture the German "volksseele": as history has demonstrated, art and politics would eventually stride side by side in Wagner's consecrated temple.

In 1848, defeated and exiled in Zurich, Wagner was poised to embark on his quarter-century creative saga, the artistic expression of his personal "Sturm und Drang" in musico-dramatic format. He concluded that humanity was in turmoil and distress because it was loveless, and had become a deceitful and treacherous world possessed by an evil lust for wealth and power. A total transformation of human nature was necessary to remedy man's aggressive power-lust: new spiritual values, and a new faith.

The underlying message of his saga would advocate the destruction of society's existing power structures and its authoritarianism in an apocalyptic cataclysm. As such, in a world reborn, humanity would be redeemed and the "man of the future" would emerge, a man of free will who would satisfy his instinctive need for mutual love and inspire fellowship. Strongly influenced by the philosophies of Feuerbach and Schopenhauer, Wagner would conclude his *Ring* with an idealistic hope for a future in which man's aggressive power-lust would gradually surrender to love, not necessarily idealized sexual love or a profound feeling of affectionate benevolence, but love that would become an active social force that advanced compassion, self-sacrifice, and creativity; humanity's survival and salvation would be achieved through a new consciousness of attitudes, beliefs, and values.

Wagner would preach his new gospel through myth, the bearer of universal themes of humanity's collective unconscious. Myths and legends represented the collective history of peoples and cultures. Although many consider myths and legends interchangeable traditions, there is definitely a distinction rooted in the respective origins of the two phenomena. Legends emanated more closely and more directly from recorded history and basically enshrine heroic deeds and events, but myths evolved the moment humanity broke from instinctive nature and rose to consciousness.

Myths served to explain the unexplainable internal and external phenomena and forces that man was unable to rationally understand; they became man's attempt to interpret "God," creation, existence, or the mechanics of natural phenomena for which there was no scientific explanation. Through myths, or the collective soul of peoples and cultures, ethical and moral foundations of societies were established.

Early Greek philosophers, as well as the Old Testament writings, speculated on the nature of the universe through myth, or in allegorical or symbolic terms and forms. The vast Greek mythology contains archetypal situations that explain the cosmos in symbolic form. Many of those myths would become merged into religion as their messages became ritualized to ensure remembrance. But from time immemorial man has created symbolism and imagery in order to recall glory, triumph, and sacred and divine acts. In myths, people, things, and events are clothed in allegory and symbolism, and achieve their greatest effect by providing multiple layers of meaning.

Wagner believed that myths represented "the poem of a life-view held in common," humanity's intuitive expression of the ultimate truths of its own nature and destiny in symbolic form. In the *Ring*, Wagner presents his pageantry of misdirected humanity within the framework of the classic German and Norse myths, extensively appropriating their symbolism, allegory and archetypes. For Wagner, myths provided universal human themes, which, he noted, were "true for all time: the distilled essence of human experience from untold generations before us."

Nevertheless, the essence of myth derives almost totally from the evocative power of its symbolism. Wagner believed strongly in what he called "the suggestive value of myth's symbols," which provided the means to arrive at "the deep truths concealed within them." Therefore, through the symbolism of myth, psychological insights are provided, as well as the means from which to transform the unconscious part of human nature into consciousness and awareness.

Wagner's purpose was not to dramatize old myths for their own sake, but to interpret through his art the elements of their meaning that he believed had relevance in his own time. As Wagner did for *Tannhäuser, Lohengrin, Tristan und Isolde*, and later *Parsifal*, he scoured the powerful German myths and legends for symbolic representational sources for his *Ring* story, ideas that he considered to be deeply ingrained in the German collective unconscious. He would reinterpret and adapt the myths in accordance with his own conceptions and creative purposes, providing meaning when he thought it was lacking, or modifying them when they seemed contradictory. Ultimately the *Ring* became a dramatic synthesis of the complex mythology of Northern Europe. Nevertheless, Wagner modernized the underlying meanings of the myths in order to reflect the destructive social and political evils of his contemporary society, evils he hoped to transform through a new world order governed by a new spiritual faith in love and compassion.

The ancient poets conveyed their symbolism through verbal imagery, and later dramatists added visual imagery. But Wagner was creating opera, the ingenious art form that conveys drama through two languages: the power of words, and the evocative power of music; words provoke thought, but music evokes feeling. Wagner's theater would provide sight and sound, but he would ritualize the symbolism of myth and add emotive power by interpreting them through musical symbolism: leitmotifs.

B etween 1848 and 1852 Wagner poured over Teutonic and Norse mythological sources to glean significant elements for *The Ring of the Nibelung*: the Norse Thidrek Saga and Eddas, and the German Völsunga and Nibelungenlied sagas. (Discounting unfortunate historical associations, "Teutonic" is not a racial but a linguistic term that identifies peoples whose languages belong to one particular group of the Indo-European family: Icelandic, Norwegian, Swedish, Danish, Frisian, Dutch, Flemish, German — and English.)

The physical ring itself became the central allegorical symbol and energetic impulse of his music drama. In Viking and Norse mythologies, magic rings were considered potent symbols of power, fortune and fame, as well as symbols of destiny; in their adverse form, if corrupted by greed, they were perceived as omens of tragedy and doom.

In all of Wagner's source sagas, three villainous forces are locked in eternal combat, all rivals to master and dominate the world: Gods, Giants, and Dwarfs. All of these forces are decadent and corrupt; in Wagner's *Ring*, they are symbolic representations of classes within the composer's 19th century contemporary society.

First, there is a race of Giants. They are symbols of the bloated bourgeoisie of Wagner's contemporary world, a class incapable of rising above the lowest form of materialism, but too indolent and too stupid to aspire to the ultimate prize of world-mastery; they desire only to live their lives in the protection and safety of their wealth.

Second, there are the Dwarfs, in particular, the evil Nibelung Dwarf Alberich, a force of unmitigated material lust who is obsessed with the acquisition of wealth and power. It is Alberich who steals the Gold in which riches and power are hidden, and by renouncing love, he is able to fashion the all-powerful Ring from the Gold, enslave the Nibelungs, and force them to amass his immense Hoard; with his newfound power Alberich intends to master the world and defeat the Gods and Giants. Alberich is the incarnation of all forces of materialism in society for whom money is synonymous with power; with his wealth, Alberich strives to become the wielder of infernal power.

Third, there are the Gods. They are the loftier spirits who bear the responsibility of rescuing the world from two threatening evils: Giants and Dwarfs. The Gods are allegorically the incarnation of corrupt nineteenth-century politicians or rulers of modern states. The Gods are ordained to use their power to maintain order and benefit the world. Wagner commented, to "bind the elements by wise laws and devote themselves to the careful nurture of the human race." But the Gods (any corrupt politician or ruler responsible for the injustices in the world) are morally flawed, unethical, and unscrupulous, achieving peace not by reconciliation and persuasion, but by force, cunning and deceit. Their supposed higher world order that is intended to evoke moral consciousness becomes absorbed by the evil against which they struggle; in the end, the Gods become as despicable and immoral as their enemies, a group who continually elevate self-interest above conscience and law.

The original Nibelungenlied deals primarily with the universal themes of lust, greed, and power. Although Wagner's ancient sources vary slightly in their specifics, certain aspects of the mythological accounts were common to all of them.

Alberich, a Dwarf, steals the Gold from the Rhine maidens, forges a Ring of power, and by upsetting the world's balance of power, incites the Gods and Giants to suppress him; after the Gods steal his Ring, he invokes a Curse on any possessor of the Ring. The Giants, Fafner and Fasolt, demand the Ring, Hoard, and Tarnhelm from the Gods in payment for building their Valhalla fortress; they carry off Freyja, the Goddess of love, as ransom. The youthful hero, Sigurd (Siegfried), slays Fafner, who had used the magic power of the Tarnhelm to transform himself into a Dragon; Sigurd acquires the Ring and the Hoard, but with it, its dooming Curse.

Sigurd falls in love with the Valkyrie, Brynhild, winning her from the fire that protected her enchanted sleep. But Grimhild, a sorceress and Queen of the Nibelungs, bewitches Sigurd into betraying Brynhild so that he can marry her daughter, Gudrun. Brynhild, now the possessor of the Ring gifted to her by Sigurd, seeks revenge and the return of her honor, but she is slain by the envious Nibelung Dwarf brothers who seek the all-powerful treasure.

In those myths, curses, magic, and sorcery represent powerful forces of doom and destiny. Heroes like Sigurd are blessed with magical weapons and arcane wisdom, and the Godhead, Odin (Wotan), is an arch-sorcerer who wanders the world disguised as a vagrant to gather information about world events (Wanderer). In some of the early sagas, the Valkyries were dark angels of death, or sinister spirits of slaughter, who soared over the battlefield like birds of prey to gather chosen heroes and bear them away to Valhalla, the heavenly fortress of Odin. In later Norse myth, the Valkyries were romanticized and became Odin's shield maidens, virgins with golden hair who served the chosen heroes mead and meat in the great hall of Valhalla. In the Volsung and Nibelungenlied sagas, the heroine Brynhild is idealized as a beautiful, fallen Valkyrie, more vulnerable than her fierce predecessors, and in many episodes, she falls in love with mortal heroes. And in the later myths, the tragedies of lovers rather than their heroic deeds are highlighted; as the hero Sigurd died, he called to his beloved Brynhild.

Thus, the Norse and German legends and myths provided Wagner with his underlying literary structure for his saga of *The Ring of the Nibelung.* Wagner would retain all of the myth's allegorical symbolism, but he would humanize their characters to make their story of lust, greed and power, a metaphor for his times.

Nevertheless, in many instances, Wagner was modifying his sources and creating a new myth. His most classic and ingenious innovations to his story were Alberich's renunciation of love that provided him with the secret to make the magic Ring from the Gold, and the introduction of Erda, the omniscient prophetess who awakens Wotan to his guilt. Wagner's original intent in *Siegfried's Death*, which ultimately became the final work, *Twilight of the Gods*, was that the sky god, Wotan, would receive Siegfried in Teutonic heaven (Valhalla), after the hero redeemed the world by transforming it into a classless society. However, Wagner could not betray his obsession with his archetypal heroines: Brünnhilde became that archetypal Wagnerian heroine, who redeems the world through her sacrificial suicide, and eliminates the Curse on the Ring by returning it to the Rhinemaidens; it is her noble sacrifice for the love of Siegfried that provides the prescription for the spiritual rebirth of the world.

In 1848, Wagner began to write a Prose Sketch entitled "The Nibelungen Myth as Scheme for a Drama," publishing it privately in 1853. By its final transformation it became a tetralogy that comprised the libretto and scenario for four music dramas: the title became *Der Ring des Nibelungen*, "The Ring of the Nibelung," or "The Nibelung's Ring." Ultimately, Wagner's four music dramas became *The Rhinegold* ("Das Rheingold"), *The Valkyrie* ("Die Walküre"), *Siegfried*, and *Twilight of the Gods* ("Götterdämmerung.")

Wagner wrote his four texts in reverse order, beginning with "Siegfried's Death," now *Twilight of the Gods*, and working backwards to explain earlier events: *Young Siegfried* became *Siegfried*, and eventually, *The Valkyrie*, and the *Prologue*, or *The Rhinegold*. Wagner himself called his epic a trilogy: a "Prologue" followed by three music dramas.

The music for *The Rhinegold* was begun in 1853, *The Valkyrie* in 1854, and *Siegfried* in 1857. But halfway through the second act of *Siegfried* Wagner laid down his pen for nine years, writing to Liszt: "I have led my Siegfried into the beautiful forest solitude. There I have left him under a linden tree and, with tears from the depths of my heart said farewell to him: he is better there than anywhere else."

Wagner had written himself to a standstill and needed stimulation from a totally different project: *Tristan und Isolde* and *Die Meistersinger* were composed during the interim. It is significant that when Wagner returned to *Siegfried*'s third act, his gear change is reflected with a blazing new creative energy: metaphorically, perhaps it represents Siegfried's — and to an extent Wagner's — rise to consciousness and awareness.

Between 1848 and 1853, as Wagner contemplated and penned the libretto for his *Ring* saga, he wrote a number of prose works; chief among them were "Art and Revolution," "The Art-Work of the Future," "Opera and Drama," and "A Communication to my Friends." In those literary works, and particularly "Opera and Drama," which essentially became the theoretical blueprint for the *Ring*, Wagner vented his struggle with contemporary opera's structure and architecture. Ultimately, he theorized new artistic impulses that drove him toward a new conception of opera: opera was to become a new form of music drama, a glorious fusion of the power of words with the emotive power of music. (Wagner never used the term "music drama," a designation applied to his theories by successors, critics, and scholars.)

Specifically, in "Opera and Drama" (1850-51), Wagner basically embellished ideas about operatic structure that were propounded earlier by Monteverdi, Gluck, and E. T. A. Hoffmann, the latter an extraordinary literary and musical genius of the nineteenth- century German Romantic period. Nevertheless, Wagner was conceiving a new type of opera that he hoped would return to the ideals of Greek drama, as he understood it: the expression of human aspirations and sensibilities in allegorical and symbolic form, and with music integrated to provide the full dramatic expression of the conflict and tension. Thus, Wagner envisioned the disappearance of the old type of opera that was structured with "set pieces" or "numbers," or musical forms that were separated by recitative or dialogue.

Wagner told a friend in 1851, "I will write no more operas"; he was announcing that as he struggled to compose the music for the *Ring* he was forced to break from traditional forms. His challenge was to let drama run an unbroken course without interrupting the action with purely musical forms (traditional arias, et al). As such, he envisioned a complete fusion of drama and music, each serving the other naturally and without artifice, but neither one constraining the other. The words had to share equally with the music in realizing the drama, and their inflections would sound ideally in alliterative clusters from which the vocal line would emerge, rising and falling with the inherent power of the words themselves. The singing voices were to give the impression of heightened speech, or "sung drama." What the sung words could not convey, the orchestra would convey through ever-recurring musical themes, what Wagner called "motifs of memory," but later termed leitmotifs.

In the *Ring* Wagner attempted to put theory into practice. Since his drama did not adapt to conventional operatic forms, there would be no self-contained numbers, solos, duets, and choruses. His scenario was a continuously flowing drama whose lines were focused, without rhyme, and often irregular in length, all seemingly formless: much of his writing favored the "Stabreim" technique, an ancient device from German and English poetry that featured assonances that provided similar sounding vowels.

His extensive use of Narratives also differed from standard operatic structures. The Narrative became an important organic part of the drama that served to elucidate and expose the plot: narratives are introspective monologues that serve to provide explanations, flashbacks and recollections. And most significantly, Wagner would elevate the emotional temperature of his drama through symphonic development of those musical "motifs of memory," thematic ideas, or leitmotifs, that would be altered and varied for psychological and dramatic impact, and reach their full expression through a woven symphonic texture.

L eitmotifs are translated in most musical guidebooks as "leading motives"; they are short, fairly simple musical phrases that describe or identify certain ideas, characters, objects, whether seen, mentioned, or thought about. Leitmotifs act as musical symbols that become engraved in the listener's memory and serve to explain, narrate, or provide psychological insight. Most significantly, when a firm relation between the leitmotif and its meaning have been established in the listener's mind it becomes a symbol that is recognized quickly and almost unconsciously through the power of association; thus, leitmotifs provide important information which can be conveyed even more effectively through the musical language. In Wagner's new musico-dramatic architecture, the musical leitmotif became the essential means to convey elements of the story; Wagner himself called them "Hauptmotiv," or principal motive, a technique which he did not invent, but certainly brought to its fullest flowering in his music dramas.

Counterpoint, or polyphony, defines one or more independent melodies, or a combination of independent melodies that are integrated or juxtaposed into a single harmonic texture. The essential ideal of the leitmotif technique was to join the themes contrapuntally, and in Wagner's particular case, present them with symphonic grandeur. Nineteenth century Romantic composers, such as Wagner, Liszt, Mendelsohn, and Brahms, revered the earlier counterpoint techniques of Palestrina and Bach. But their true inclination was toward combinations of leitmotifs; Franz Schubert's lieder songs, and those of Hugo Wolf, were highly innovative because their accompaniments contained motives that interacted contrapuntally with the vocal parts. In Wagner's new music drama style he was striving toward an ideal of "sung drama," or the imitation of speech through music; in its perfect manifestation it was "speech-song," or "Sprechgesang," which he contrapuntally balanced with motives in the orchestral accompaniment.

The great virtue of leitmotifs is that they work on multiple levels: they not only foreshadow the future, but by evoking the past they can provide the present with an infinitely greater immediacy. As an example, in *Twilight of the Gods*, Siegfried does not recall his life before his death. It is after his death, in the Funeral music, that the entire panorama of Siegfried's life is revealed; but it is revealed through music. While the vassals carry Siegfried to the Hall of the Gibichungs, the entire *Ring* saga seems to pass in review. Thus, through already familiar musical motives Wagner recalls all the important moments of Siegfried's life, urging the listener through music to remember the Volsungs, Wotan's children whom he created to resolve the wretched dilemma of the Cursed Ring, Siegmund and Sieglinde's love and its bitter pain, the divine Sword which Wotan had driven into the tree for Siegmund to claim in his moment of need, and remembrances that Siegmund and Sieglinde produced Siegfried, the hero whose destiny it was to wed the omniscient Brünnhilde. The contrapuntal fusion and skillful harmonic interweaving and variation of leitmotifs convey powerful emotions: it ultimately becomes the orchestra that develops these reminiscences in accordance with the expressive need of the dramatic and psychological action, and Wagner, the quintessential symphonist, ingeniously achieves the full embodiment of the leitmotif technique in the *Ring* through his orchestra.

The *Ring*'s four music dramas are united by related musical material; some two hundred leitmotifs represent a massive vocabulary of musico-dramatic symbols and associations. By the time of the final episode, *Twilight of the Gods*, the listener can virtually follow the dramatic narrative by interpreting the meaning of its musical leitmotif symbols without the benefit of visual or verbal clarification. As such, Wagner's orchestra functions like a massive Greek chorus that narrates and comments on the action. In the *Ring*, Wagner proved his genius as both music dramatist and symphonist, composing elements in the music drama that have become indelible for the listener: *The Rhinegold*'s scene transitions and the "Rainbow Bridge" finale, *The Valkyrie*'s "Ride of the Valkyries" and "Fire music," *Twilight of the God*'s "Rhine Journey" and "Funeral music," and after Brünnhilde's "Immolation," the orchestral depiction of the downfall of the gods and the world's redemption.

Allegory denotes symbolic representation. The *Ring*'s leitmotifs are specifically symbolic representations, but they are presented in the language of music. It is through the emotive power of the musical language that ideas in the *Ring* are conveyed and responses are evoked; as such, the drama's characters, elements, and events become part of a complete mythography whose inner allegorical symbolism, in both words and music, provide intensely profound understanding as well as different levels of meaning. The symbolism of myth evokes intuitive rather than rational responses from the human psyche; Wagner's musical leitmotifs become those same symbolic images, often revealing and evoking profound inner thoughts and emotions. Ultimately, leitmotifs provided Wagner with the organic structure for his music drama, but more importantly, they provided the wherewithal to add profound impact to the drama through musical symbolism.

Wagner was a man possessing profound intellectual curiosity; he was a voracious reader whose huge library of books, abandoned at the time of his 1848 exile, remains in Dresden. The *Ring* consumed Wagner over a vast creative period of 26 years, and inevitably, certain ideological conceptions of his massive undertaking were bound to change.

Initially, Wagner's sole intent in the *Ring* was to express his moral outrage at the evil values of his contemporary society: in metaphorical or allegorical form, he would parade all the decadent, degenerate, and philistine protagonists of his contemporary world, and ultimately destroy them in a cataclysmic apocalypse of fire and water. And, the victorious hero, Siegfried, would then succeed to Valhalla after recreating the world into a classless society. But over time, Wagner had evolved from the impassioned revolutionary of Dresden. Intuitively and rationally, he began to develop a different philosophical context for his saga that transcended the passions of his original cri de coeur and Sturm and Drang.

The German philosopher, Arthur Schopenhauer, had come under the spell of Orientalism when early in life he stumbled into a French translation of the Indian Upanishads; he became enthralled with Hindu and Buddhist doctrines regarding renunciation of the Will, or the extinguishing of desire. In "The World as Will and Idea" (1818), Schopenhauer pitted Eastern mystical conceptions of wisdom against the Enlightenment's faith in reason, science, and civilization. Although his book remained unread for some 40 years, Europe's disillusionment after the 1848 Revolutions brought him a new and enthusiastic audience.

Schopenhauer directed his radical views about the renunciation of human Will to both Enlightenment and Christian ideology. In his conception, the Enlightenment had created a false optimism through its empty faith in reason and progress. He also condemned Christianity, which he concluded had urged men to strive for salvation in this world through a set of religious and moral preconceptions, which, he argued, posed the illusion of "Will as idea." Schopenhauer reasoned that the ultimate reality was that the exercise of human Will was purposeless, aimless, and neither reasonable nor rational: Will was simply a blindness that urged man to strive for meaningless goals such as their lust for wealth and power, and their achievement would ultimately cause anguish.

Schopenhauer proposed that man had to escape from the sickness and curse of the Will, a yearning that imprisoned him in a fatal state of eternal desire; they represented urges that man must extinguish, abandon, and renounce. Schopenhauer envisioned a new way of understanding the world that was immune from the remorseless desires of the ego, what he termed the destructive idea of the "world as Will." His resolution of the dilemma was for man to achieve salvation not through a religious or spiritual path, but through philosophic knowledge, compassion, and sympathy for others. And more importantly, that man could obtain a momentary release from life's curse of desire through aesthetic experience, such as viewing a painting or listening to a symphony; by experiencing the world in a new way — through moments of pure contemplation of art and music — man would become uncorrupted by contact with the gross materialism that surrounded him.

Schopenhauer's conception that music and art provided a way to transcend the Will's relentless grip — albeit temporarily — coincided with Wagner's belief that his music dramas would provide relief for restless souls. But Schopenhauer added intellectual profundity to Wagner's vision, and armed with his new philosophy, the composer became more convinced than ever that his music dramas would become a consecrated art form, and therefore, a transcendent musical experience.

In 1854, while Wagner was composing the music to the second act of *The Valkyrie*, he was deeply engrossed in Wotan's torment, an agony that was caused by the frustration of the Godhead's Will. Simultaneously, Wagner became immersed in the spell of Schopenhauer's philosophy, the idea that all human anxiety and conflict derived from self-imposed desires, or Will. Wagner began to realize what he had felt intuitively; that Wotan's inner conflicts derived from the frustration of his Will.

Wagner became mesmerized — and totally indoctrinated — by Schopenhauer's philosophy. He realized that the "renunciation of Will" had been a theme he had subconsciously brought to the surface in his earlier *The Flying Dutchman* and *Tannhäuser;* the idea that the world of active desire resulted in a suffering from which the soul yearned to be freed, and that freedom could only be achieved when the Will was extinguished. Later, Wagner's *Tristan und Isolde* (1863) became a testament to Schopenhauer's philosophy. (Wagner became so engrossed in Schopenauerian philosophy, that he contemplated the opera, *Der Sieger*, a story centering on a disciple of Buddha.)

By applying Schopenhauer's philosophy of the "renunciation of Will," the essential conflicts of the *Ring* saga developed more profound meaning. Wagner had by now concluded that industrialized Europe would never escape or find release from its struggles:

"I saw that the world was Nichtigkeit, a nothingness or an illusion." Thus, the *Ring*'s power conflicts were incontrovertible elements in the world's evolution, but he was now convinced more than ever that their cause was specifically humanity's blind exercise of Will.

Armed with Schopenhauer's preaching, Wagner found it necessary to revise his original conception for the conclusion of the *Ring,* and decided that it was necessary to destroy Wotan and the Gods in the final moments of *Twilight of the Gods.* Wagner commented about the fall of the Gods: "The necessity for the downfall of the Gods springs from our innermost feelings, as it does from the innermost feelings of Wotan. It is important to justify the necessity by feeling, for Wotan who has risen to the tragic height of willing his own downfall."

The Godhead Wotan had evolved into the indisputable tragic character of the *Ring* story, his agony the result of his insatiable Will as master the world. For Wagner, it was now necessary to conclude the *Ring* with the Schopenhauerian "renunciation of Will," a decisive condemnation of Wotan's Will — and all human Will — that he now believed was the cause of the world's evil. And similarly, Brünnhilde's sacrificial suicide and the purification of the Ring's Curse, would represent an acceptance of fate that finally released humanity from its endless cycle of desire, rebirth, and death: the ultimate conclusion of the *Ring,* like *Tristan und Isolde,* became an expression of pure Schopenhauerian philosophy.

Brünnhilde is the true heroine of the *Ring*, the synthesis of all of the Romantic era's ideals of love, wisdom, sacrifice, and redemption. Romanticists, and particularly Wagner, believed that man's most profound desire was to desperately seek human warmth and affection, and to give love and be understood through love: love was deemed the noble spirit that sustained the world and illuminated every human soul.

The keystone of all Wagner's operas is that man is ultimately redeemed through human love, an alternative path to salvation and redemption, that, like religious spirituality, raised consciousness to greater emotional and aesthetic sensibilities. But it was Goethe's ideal of the ennobled "holy woman" whom the Romanticists sought in their passionate pursuit of man's love-ideal: it was Goethe's glorification of the "eternal female" at the conclusion of *Faust*, "Das Ewig-weibliche zieht uns hinan" ("The eternal feminine draws us onward"), that became the rallying cry of German Romanticism; she was that intuitive, sacrificing woman whose love, understanding and wisdom provided the glorious path to man's redemption.

Goethe's eternal female became Wagner's "woman of the future," or "femme eterne," who, like Beethoven's Leonora in *Fidelio*, became the model for his idealized heroines: Senta (*The Flying Dutchman*), Elisabeth (*Tannhäuser*), Brünnhilde (*The Ring of the Nibelung*), and Isolde (*Tristan und Isolde*). These sacrificing women essentially provide unquestioning and unconditional love; as such, they redeem and heal man from his narcissism, ego, loneliness, isolation, desires, needs, and yearnings. Ultimately, the German Romanticists — and particularly Wagner — believed that man may strive through art or reason toward a synthesis of human experience, but it was woman's love alone that would lead him to achieving life's ultimate fulfillment. So for Wagner, woman's unqualified, sacrificing love became the ideal: in *The Flying Dutchman*, the condemned, egocentric, almost Byronesque Dutchman is redeemed through Senta's love, compassion, and ultimately her sacrifice; in *Tannhäuser*, the errant and tormented minstrel is redeemed not through his Pope, but through the love and sacrifice of Elisabeth.

The ultimate evil in the *Ring* is not necessarily Wotan's duplicity, but Alberich's renunciation of love, his negation of humanity's most profound aspiration; the entire drama concludes with the affirmation of the healing power of love. Therefore, Brünnhilde becomes the glorified heroine of the *Ring,* the idealized eternal female or "holy woman" whose insight, wisdom and love redeem the world by cleansing it from its Curse of evil.

Brünnhilde is that heroic female force that integrates all of man's yearnings. It is her love and wisdom that energizes Siegfried and raises him to consciousness, and she alone reconciles all the conflicts of the *Ring* through her sacrifice. In the finale of the *Ring*, the sacrificial consummation of her holy marriage is a magical moment that summarizes the entire essence of German Romanticism's eternal woman. Brünnhilde calls out to her magic steed, Grane: "Do you know where we go together? Does the fire's light on Siegfried draw you to it too? Siegfried, Siegfried, see how your holy wife greets you!"

Brünnhilde's immolation is a shattering moment, but a momentous affirmation of love as the world becomes purified from its Curse. Wagner seizes this moment as his music relentlessly modulates and interweaves significant leitmotifs, all triumphantly surging toward the towering prophecy of the world's transformation: Siegfried's heroic music fuses with the motive of the Fall of the Gods, and the motive of Redemption through Love provides the final transcendence. The Rhine banks flood, the flames ebb, and Hagen, whose monomania remains undaunted, plunges into the Rhine to seize the Ring, but is dragged to its depths by the Rhinemaidens. The Rhinemaidens reveal the Ring they have recaptured from Brünnhilde's ashes, now purified from its Curse. Above, Valhalla is ablaze, Wotan waiting for the transforming fires to destroy the Gods and end the old order.

The cataclysm does not signal the end of humanity, but rather, provides a glimmer of hope that suggests that a new generation will arise and be stirred to greatness through love and compassion: one cycle of humanity ended; another is ready to begin.

Wagner's *Ring* relates a profound story about crisis within the human soul, a portrait of that eternal conflict between nature and human nature.

Man is the maker of myths; *The Ring of the Nibelung* is Wagner's myth. In myths, human nature is ambivalent, a creature who is both great and flawed as he struggles between goodness and his destructive impulses. The *Ring* reaches deep into the abyss of the human soul, and in the end concludes that man indeed possesses the propensity for greatness, a grandeur he can achieve when his energies are transformed toward love and elevated moral conscience.

The evil Gods in the *Ring* acted to possess rather than protect, to conquer rather than to defend. The Gods were ordained to protect the world against evil, but when malevolent forces stole the secret of the Ring's power and threatened their power, the Gods became flawed, toppling the moral and ethical scales by becoming as deceitful and treacherous as the evil they were ordained to control. The peace that they presumed to have maintained was not achieved by persuasion and reconciliation, but by criminal acts involving force and guile; ultimately they sacrificed their morality for their own self-serving needs. Wagner cited their hypocrisy in his Prose Sketch, "The purpose of their higher world order is moral consciousness, but the wrong against which they fight attaches to themselves."

The human conflicts portrayed in the *Ring* are universal and timeless, a view into the human soul that possesses almost Biblical grandeur: avarice, greed, duplicity, fear, treachery and betrayal, incest, murder, hatred, and compassion and love. Wagner's *Ring* is a journey into the human soul. But the *Ring* portrays its conflicting landscape in the language of music, an evocative force that transcends the power of words and reaches into the very depths of the human soul, arousing and awakening emotions and sensibilities that are at times repressed in the dark human unconscious.

In the final moments of *Twilight of the Gods*, Wagner the poet was in conflict with Wagner the music dramatist; ultimately, he relied on his music to convey what the poet was trying to express in words. Originally, Wagner intended the omniscient Brünnhilde to utter a profound ode to love, but he decided to leave the gravity of those final moments to his musical language. Wagner's concluding music portrays a collision between all the conflicting forces of the *Ring*. Yet, his final musical statement is one of love, compassion and hope, a spiritual message proclaiming that universal faith in human love will elevate conscience, and promote those enduring ideals of wisdom, character, humility, courage, civility, and justice; the ultimate ideals necessary for humanity to survive.

Wagner commented on the entire essence of the *Ring*: "Every human being must be capable of feeling this unconsciously and of instinctively putting it into practice." ("Opera and Drama")

A Prologue to the *Prologue*

As *The Rhinegold* unfolds, its first 136 measures suggest the world's creation; it portrays a primordial wasteland of water in which surging arpeggios convey the water's flow and unceasing rise. Wagner was said to have remarked to Franz Liszt that his opening for *The Rhinegold* was like "the beginning of the world."

Wagner's Teutonic and Norse sources for *The Ring of the Nibelung* contained a "genesis," a creation myth that explained the formation of the elements and the principal inhabitants of the world: Gods, Giants, and Dwarfs. With minor variations, those myths explain that in the beginning there was neither sea nor shore, nor heaven nor earth, but only Ginnungagap, a vast "yawning abyss" or "emptiness," which lay between the realms of fire and freezing cold. After fire melted the ice, warm air from the south collided with the chill from the north causing drops of moisture to fall into the gaping chasm of Ginnungagap. Over time, drops in the chasm caused more ice to melt, and the first life form evolved: Audhumla, the primeval cow.

From Audhumla's tears "flowed four rivers of milk" that nurtured Ymir, who was the first frost Giant, the implacable enemy of the Gods. Audhumla licked the salty ice that ultimately released Borr, or Buri. Borr married Bestla, the daughter of a frost Giant, and had three sons: Odin (Wotan), Vili, and Ve. The sons battled incessantly against the Giants. Finally, they slew Ymir, and then hurled his body into the center of the Ginnungagap.

Ymir's body gave birth to the world; his flesh became the earth, his bones formed the mountains, his teeth formed the rocks and stones, his hair formed the trees, his blood turned into the lakes and seas, and his skull formed the sky. Four Dwarfs, Nordi, Sudri, Austri, and Westri, were formed from maggots in the rotting flesh of the slain giant, and then were condemned to life underground. Ymir's wounds flooded the land and drowned all his frost children, except his grandson, Bergelmir, who escaped with his wife and propagated the race of Giants.

The fierce Wotan made the human race from Ymir's body, which then inhabited the Midgard. But wars raged across the birthing world. Borr's sons, led by the Godhead Wotan, struggled against the Giants. Wotan loved battle, and was the esteemed father of slain heroes, his name akin to fury or madness. He inspired men into battle by rousing them into a frenzied rage that caused them to fear nothing and feel no pain. Wotan and the Gods raised a Hall of the Valiant, Valhalla, to which Valkyries would take the bravest human warriors after they were slain in battle. In Valhalla, the God presided over the resuscitated and resurrected heroes.

The Germanic Gods feared their doom, a final struggle between the Gods and the forces of evil that would resolve in a cosmic apocalypse; a "twilight of the gods," or Ragnarok. The catastrophe of the Ragnarok was inevitable and unpreventable, but did not signal the end of the cosmos: a new world was destined to rise again because two humans had taken shelter in Yggdrasil, the sacred tree of wisdom and knowledge; they emerged after the apocalypse and repopulated the earth.

Wotan's Spear represents the symbol of his moral power; on its shaft he engraved the Laws of human conduct. Wotan sacrificed an eye after he drank from the Well of Wisdom, symbolically turning inward and cultivating his soul with wisdom and knowledge;

these were his first steps in the acquisition of consciousness and Will. Like Prometheus who daringly stole fire for mankind, and Adam who ate the apple that brought knowledge, it was Wotan's drinking from the Well of Wisdom that represented his self-emancipation from nature and the end of innocence. In his new state of consciousness and separation from nature, he embarked on humanity's eternal struggle to control the forces of good and evil.

But in Wotan's new state of consciousness, he exercised his Will to control, rule, and even exploit the world. Wagner commented on Wotan's "sin" against nature and his rise to consciousness: "But error is the father of knowledge, and the history of the beginning of knowledge and error is the history of the human race, from the myths of earlier times down to the present day."

The Rhinegold

("Das Rheingold")

Music drama with a *Prelude* and four scenes

Music composed by Richard Wagner

Drama written by Richard Wagner

Premiere: Hoftheater in Munich, 1869

The Rhinegold **is the first music drama, or** *Prologue,* **to the**
The Ring of the Nibelung **("Der Ring des Nibelungen")**

Principal Characters in The Rhinegold

Gods:

Wotan, the Godhead	Bass-baritone
Fricka, wife of Wotan, and Goddess of marriage	Mezzo-soprano
Loge, God of fire	Tenor
Freia, Goddess of eternal youth, sister of Fricka	Soprano
Donner, God of thunder, wind, lightning, and brother of Fricka	Baritone
Froh, God of fields and rain, and brother of Fricka	Tenor
Erda, Goddess of wisdom	Contralto

Nibelung Dwarfs:

Alberich, a smith	Baritone
Mime, brother of Alberich, a smith	Tenor

Giants:

Fasolt, brother of Fafner	Bass
Fafner, brother of Fasolt	Bass

Rhinemaidens:

Woglinde	Soprano
Wellgunde	Mezzo-soprano
Flosshilde	Mezzo-soprano

Story Narrative with Music Highlight Examples

Prelude:

The Prelude portrays a primordial wasteland at the beginning of creation that is dominated by water. Water is a primal element from which, science claims, all life evolved. In the musical introduction, the Rhine's waters gain strength and motion, and surging musical arpeggios suggest the water's flow and unceasing movement. As Wagner remarked to Franz Liszt, the musical imagery of the Prelude portrays "the beginning of the world."

The Waters of the Rhine

Scene 1: *In the depths of the Rhine.*

The misty lower depths of the Rhine are saturated with rock fissures and crags. Woglinde, a Rhinemaiden, greets the waters while swimming gracefully around a large rock whose peak is clearly visible in the upper waters. The Rhinemaidens praise the newborn world with childlike innocence and awe.

Greeting the Waters

Wei - a! Wa - ga! Wo-ge,, du Wel - le, wal-le zur Wie - ge!
Weia! Waga! Woge! Wandering waters, swing us in our cradle!

Woglinde's sister Rhinemaidens, Wellgunde and Flosshilde frolic merrily, but Flosshilde chides them for their carelessness in maintaining their vigil on the sleeping Gold which they protect.

While the Rhinemaidens delight in their innocent diversion, the hunchbacked Nibelung Dwarf, Alberich, emerges from a dark cavern and watches their frolicking with ever-increasing pleasure. He calls out to the Rhinemaidens, announcing that he comes from Nibelheim, the darkest caverns of the earth, which he would gladly abandon if he could share their merriment and love. The Rhinemaidens recoil and elude the unsavory visitor, mocking and rejecting him with heartless contempt, while reminding each other that their father warned them to beware of such ugly and repulsive creatures.

When Alberich pursues the Rhinemaidens lustily, they taunt and tease him, causing sensations of love and desire to become stirred within him. When he tries to grasp one of the Rhinemaidens, he slips awkwardly on the slimy crags, prompting the maiden's laughter. Frustrated, his desires transform into bitterness. He loses his temper and condemns all of them, concluding that love will always elude him. Nevertheless, he continues to pursue them with a sensual fury, their defiance and evasion compounding his avenging passions: in his frustrated fury, he calls them "cold and bony fish" who should "take eels for their lovers."

Flosshilde pretends to take pity on the Dwarf and disarms him with cajolery and deception, promising him that he will be more successful with her than with her sisters; with her, he will enjoy the passions of genuine love. With feigned compliments, she tells Alberich, "Oh, the sting of your glance and your stiff scrubby beard, I would like to feel it forever! And might the locks of your hair, so shaggy and wild, float around Flosshilde forever! And your toad's shape and the croak of your voice! Oh, might I be dazzled and amazed to see and hear nothing else but these!"

Flosshilde heartlessly continues to taunt the Dwarf by first embracing him, and then brusquely rejecting him, prompting her sisters to burst into raucous laughter. Alberich becomes totally discouraged and enraged, vowing to seize at least one of them. As they elude him, he again slips awkwardly on the rocks. Derided and rejected, Alberich explodes in a fury, and then vengefully shakes his menacing fist at the Rhinemaidens.

Alberich's attention is suddenly drawn to a dazzling, radiant glow that he perceives in the waters above; it is the sleeping Rhinegold awakening.

The Sleeping Rhinegold

The Rhinemaiden's swim around the Gold gracefully, praising its radiance with joy and rapture.

The Rhinegold

Rhein - gold! Rhein - gold! Leuchtende Lust,   wie lach'st du so hell und hehr!
Rhinegold! Rhinegold! Radiant joy, who laughs in glorious light!

Alberich, struck with awe, inquires about the Gold's significance. The Rhinemaidens invite him to join them to praise its magnificence, but he rejects their childish games. Nevertheless, he becomes aroused when they assure him that the Gold possesses limitless powers, and that anyone who wins the Gold and fashions a Ring from it would become master of the world.

The Ring

Flosshilde then admonishes her sisters for their indiscretion, reminding them that their father warned them to guard the Gold carefully lest some robber seize it, create a powerful Ring, and use its powers for evil. But Wellgunde and Woglinde express their confidence that they have nothing to fear from this lascivious, lusting imp, a man who is visibly tormented and too preoccupied with his passion for love: they conclude that he would certainly never renounce love to obtain the secret to master a Ring from the Gold. Woglinde then reveals the secret inherent in the Gold: "He who the power of love forswears, from all delights of love forbears."

Renunciation of Love

WOGLINDE

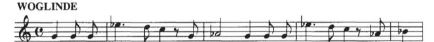

Nur wer der Min - ne Macht ent - sagt,   nur wer der Lie - be Lust ver - jagt,
He who the power of love forswears, from all delights of love forbears,

Confidently, the Rhinemaidens assure themselves that no one in all creation would ever renounce the delights of love. Ironically, they invite Alberich to join them in their merriment, for the Gold's radiance even seems to have improved the imp's hideous form. Meanwhile, the spurned Alberich's bitterness transforms into hope as his eyes remain fixed solidly on the Gold, his devious mind contemplating the hidden secrets of wealth and power that he could obtain if he renounced love and fashioned the all-powerful Ring from the treasure: "Could I, through your magic, win the world's wealth for my own? If love is to be denied me, shall my cunning win me the Gold's delight? Keep mocking me! The Nibelung comes near your toy!"

Alberich cannot master the inner world of his yearnings and desires, but he can master the external world with Gold and power. Propelled by his lust for greed and power, Alberich reconciles himself to his newfound destiny. With a demonic laugh, he springs toward the summit of the rock and stretches out his hand towards the Gold. Solemnly and triumphantly, he rises to his destiny and renounces love: "My hand quenches your light. I wrest the Gold from the rock, and will fashion the Ring of revenge. Hear me flooded waters: henceforth love shall be accursed forever!"

The Rhinemaidens scatter in terror. Alberich seizes the Gold and plunges with it into the depths of the Rhine. As he disappears from sight, his sinister mocking laughter is heard against the lamenting cries of the Rhinemaidens.

Scene 2: On a mountain height

As day dawns, the waves of the Rhine gradually transform into clouds. A fine mist slowly disperses to reveal a bright, open area atop a mountain. Visible in the background is the majestic, newly built fortress of Valhalla. In the foreground Wotan, the Godhead, and Fricka, his wife and Goddess of marriage, sleep on a flowery bank; between them and the fortress the broad Rhine flows.

Wotan dreams blissfully of the splendid fortress that has been built for the Gods; a majestic, impregnable stronghold and testament to his power from where he will rule the world with might and eternal glory. He conceived the citadel in his dreams and caused its completion through his undaunted Will.

Valhalla

Fricka, like Wotan, is a moral paradox. Although in her role of Goddess she represents moral conscience, she is not free of ordinary human weaknesses. She does not share her husband's illusions about power, for what fills him with pride, overcomes her with fear and dread. She rouses Wotan from what she calls his "deceptive dream," exhorting him to become realistic about the crisis she senses will soon overcome the Gods.

Fricka is perturbed because Wotan failed to consult with her and the other Gods before making what she considered a ludicrous contract with the Giants to build Valhalla. Wotan callously and capriciously promised to pay the Giants with Freia, her sister and the Goddess of love, whose golden apples sustain the Gods' eternal youth. Fricka chides Wotan for his heartlessness and levity in sacrificing the Goddess of love and youth for "the garish toy of empire and power."

Wotan assuages his wife's anxiety, assuring her that in truth he never intended — nor does he intend — to surrender Freia to the Giants; after all, Freia's golden apples provide eternal youth to the Gods.

Wotan's Laws, Treaties, and Compacts

Wotan calms Fricka's fears, admonishing her that he has entrusted Loge, the cunning and unscrupulous God of fire, to fulfill his promise to find an alternative payment to the Giants when the hour of reckoning arose. He regards the Giants with contempt, considering them coarse and physically repulsive creatures of low intelligence, but good laborers. He further reproaches Fricka's hypocrisy, reminding her that she indeed favored the building of Valhalla. Weren't Fricka's motivations self-serving? Didn't she believe that the new fortress would keep her errant and philandering husband at home?

Marital Fidelity

FRICKA

Herrliche   Wohnung, wonniger Hausrath,sollten dich binden zu säumender Rast.
Great halls, graces of homelife, surely should bind you peacefully.

As they speak, Wotan's sister-in-law Freia arrives, breathless and frightened.

Freia

Terrified, Freia pleads with Wotan and Fricka for help. Now that Valhalla is finished, the Giants want their pay, and Freia is defenseless against the Giants who are pursuing her. Wotan calms her fears with assurances that Loge will soon arrive to resolve the problem of payment to the Giants.

Fricka scornfully reproaches Wotan for his continued trust in that despicable trickster who has continually caused harm to the Gods. Wotan defends Loge, self-assured in his confidence that when wisdom fails, the intelligent Loge's artfulness and cunning will succeed. Wotan continues to have unbounded faith in the wily rogue. After all, although Loge initially advised him to pledge Freia to the Giants in payment for Valhalla, he also assured Wotan that he would find the means to annul the promise.

Freia, convinced that Wotan is sacrificing her to the Giants, calls desperately for help from her brothers, Donner and Froh. Fricka compounds Freia's distress by telling her somberly that the Godhead has woven a net of treachery about her and has forsaken her.

The Giants, Fasolt and Fafner, arrive, treading noisily while brandishing large clubs.

Giants

Fasolt seems gentler in nature than his fiercer brother, Fafner, and genuinely has tender feelings for Freia. Fafner, who is more uncouth and brutish than his brother, envisions Freia for what she represents: the assurance of eternal youth. Fasolt respectfully and patiently requests Freia as their promised payment, explaining that the Giants toiled endlessly, and untiringly piled heavy stones upon heavy stones in order to build Valhalla.

Wotan contemptuously refuses their demand for Freia. He denounces their request as ludicrous and asks them to suggest another payment. Fasolt becomes confounded, and inquires if the solemn Laws engraved on Wotan's Spear are nothing more than a mockery. But Fafner, more realistic, sneeringly advises his brother that the Godhead's failure to honor their contract is another example of his unscrupulousness.

Solemnly, Fasolt warns Wotan of the consequences if he fails to honor their agreement, reminding the God that his power rests in his virtue in honoring his treaties; if he renounces his promise, his wisdom shall be cursed, and the peace between the Giants and the Gods will end forever. Wotan waves Fasolt's admonition airily aside, telling him that the contract for Freia was made in jest; certainly boors like the Giants are unable to appreciate the beautiful Goddess's charm and grace.

Angrily, Fasolt accuses Wotan of mocking them. He repeats their agreement, explaining that they toiled hard solely because they wanted the reward of a beautiful woman and her assurance of eternal youth. As Fasolt speaks of Freia's charm and grace, his coarseness transforms into tenderness. But the more brutal Fafner interjects contemptuously, admonishing his brother to cease arguing with this arrogant and unscrupulous God: they will take Freia, and the Gods will be doomed, because without Freia's youth-perpetuating golden Apples the Gods will age, weaken, wither and die.

Freia's Golden Apples

Gold' - ne Äp - fel   wachsen   in   ih   - rem Gar - ten,
Golden apples bloom in her garden.

Wotan becomes restless, fearful and anxious, wondering why Loge has not arrived yet to resolve his dilemma. Meanwhile, he again asks the Giants to demand another wage, but Fasolt again refuses. As both Giants try to seize Freia, she runs to her brothers, Donner and Froh. Froh, the God of fields and rain, places a protecting arm around Freia, and Donner, the God of thunder, stands before the Giants, brandishing his hammer and threatening to strike them. Freia continues to complain that the Gods have forsaken her. Wotan intervenes and commands all to cease their quarreling. He places his Spear between the disputants and implores the Giants to trust him by assuring them that he is bound by the rules of his Law-laden Spear; if he were to break a single Treaty, his power would be ended forever.

Wotan's Spear

Angry, disgusted and frustrated, Wotan looks anxiously toward the valley for the arrival of Loge. Suddenly, he sees a sparkle of flame, and then a nimble figure that approaches, leaping from one rock to another.

Loge: the crafty demi-God

Wotan sighs in relief as Loge finally arrives.

Loge is the son of Giants, and therefore, a half-God, or demi-God; he refers to himself in relation to the Gods as "half as glorious as you glorious ones!"

As the God of fire, Loge is the patron of smiths, and the servant of man needing the benefits of fire. Loge is cunning, artful, and full of malicious mischief, a restless, elusive spirit, who sweeps homeless through the world, wandering wherever his whims lead him.

Loge remains seemingly detached from the struggle between Gods, Giants, and Dwarfs, and expresses no outward ambition for power. He prefers to remain aloof from the Gods so that he can be an objective moral mirror of their consciences.

Loge represents pure intelligence, an attribute that enables him to see issues with clarity. As such, of all the Gods, Wotan seems to be his only friend, and most in need of his talents.

Wotan confronts Loge to fulfill his promise to find a substitute payment to the Giants instead of Freia. Loge glibly raises his hands in cynical protest, denying that he made any such promises. Wotan reproves Loge's elusiveness, roguishness, and trickery, cautioning him that he should beware not to deceive him. The duplicitous Loge protests that all he had promised was that he would ponder the problem and consider a solution. Nevertheless, he has truly devoted his serious energy to resolving their problem, searching unceasingly through the world for a substitute ransom for Freia that might satisfy the Giants.

The Gods react to Loge's explanation with skepticism. Fricka angrily reproaches Wotan for placing faith in this treacherous knave; Froh tells him that he should be called "not Loge but Lüge" ("lies"); and Donner threateningly vows to destroy his power. Wotan steps between the feuding Gods and Loge to make peace, and diplomatically admonishes them not to affront his friend; after all, he assures them, the slower he is to give counsel, the craftier his insight and advice. Loge, however, remains contemptuous, claiming that their accusations against him are merely subterfuges for their own gross duplicity.

Loge then proceeds to relate the events surrounding Alberich's theft of the Rhinegold. The sorrowful Rhinemaidens told him how the Nibelung Dwarf, having sought their favors in vain, solemnly renounced love so he could fashion the all-powerful Ring, and then robbed them of the Gold; with Alberich's newfound power, he has enslaved the Nibelung Dwarfs and forced them to mine his Hoard from the Gold. The Rhinemaidens implored Loge to seek Wotan's help in punishing the thief, recover their Gold, and return it to the waters from where it had been ravished. Loge proudly compliments his integrity; he has kept his promise to the Rhinemaidens and has related their loss and grief to the Gods.

But Wotan is indifferent to Loge's story, and at this time, he is more concerned with his own pressing needs to find an alternative to pay the Giants than with the Rhinemaiden's dilemma of their ravished Gold. However, Loge's revelation about the stolen Gold does provoke and unsettle the Giants: Fasolt condemns the Nibelung Dwarf as their enemy, and one who has always evaded their grasp; Fafner expresses his conviction that with the Dwarf's newfound powers, he will be brewing mischief for all of them.

Capriciously, Fricka asks if the Gold provides adornment for women. Loge, with his usual craftiness, explains that the woman who possesses the Nibelung's golden trinkets could ensure her husband's faithfulness. Loge's revelation prompts Fricka's enthusiasm. Motivated by the fact that the Gold might provide a possible solution to her marital problems, she turns to Wotan and urges him to win the treasure.

Loge further explains that because Alberich has fashioned the all-powerful Ring, he is impregnable and beyond their reach. Loge's revelation causes fear and terror to overcome the Gods: Donner predicts that they will all become enslaved by the Dwarf Alberich if the Ring is not wrested from him; Wotan fully recognizes the ominous power Alberich now possesses; and Froh expresses his confidence that the Gods can seize the Ring from Alberich.

Loge concurs with Froh and proposes his plan: "By theft! What a thief stole, you can steal from the thief. Could anything be clearer? But Alberich guards himself with cunning weapons; to return the lustrous Gold to the Rhinemaidens, you must be shrewd and wary in order to surpass his wiles." Wotan echoes Loge with an expression of disbelief: "Return it to the Maidens?" Fricka, the Goddess of marriage, supports the Gods contemplation of theft, renouncing the ugly brood of Dwarfs who have used their wiles to lure so many women unwillingly to their lair.

Suddenly, all the Gods become silent. Each ponders their reasons and willingness to become an accomplice in forcibly wresting the Gold and Ring from Alberich, except for Wotan, who is unconvinced and expresses his reservations, fearful of achieving their goals through wrongdoing.

The Giants intervene in the Gods' dilemma: Fafner announces that the Gold would be a better alternative as payment to the Giants than Freia. Although Fasolt is initially unwilling to surrender his dreams of possessing the gracious and beautiful Freia, both

Giants trudge before Wotan and announce their decision; they will relinquish their claim to Freia if they are paid with the Nibelung's Gold.

Wotan indignantly protests that their request is ludicrous. How could he pay them with Gold that he does not own? And further, do they expect him to conquer Alberich, seize the Gold, and then casually deliver the treasure to the Giants? Wotan despairs, realizing that satisfying the Giants by conquering the Nibelung represents a distasteful and unjust solution to his dilemma.

But the God is caught in a trap, the result of his own carelessness, disingenuousness, and duplicity. In truth, Wotan never intended to surrender Freia because he trusted Loge's craftiness to find him an alternative payment. His sole purpose in making the contract with the Giants had been to fulfill his lofty dream to build Valhalla, a fortress from which he would maintain order in the world by bending both the Giants and Nibelungs to his Will. But now Wotan fears that the Dwarf Alberich threatens him — and peace in the world — and will use the Ring to master the universe. Wotan becomes convinced that Alberich must be defeated, and that the Gods are justified in using force and deceit: he must fight fire with fire and evil with evil; a sacrifice of conscience and justice that he must make for the greater good of the world.

Suddenly, Fasolt brusquely draws Freia to his side and orders her to remain with them until the ransom of Alberich's Gold is paid. Freia will remain their hostage until nightfall, and if the Nibelung's Gold is not tendered to them by that time, the Gods will forfeit her forever. Freia is thrown across their shoulders and screams in vain for help as she is dragged away.

As Freia disappears, the Gods suddenly transform, becoming old and pale, seemingly sick, wrinkled and withered. Froh's boldness and courage desert him; Donner's arms become feeble and he is unable to hold his great hammer; and Fricka has now grown old and gray.

Cynically and unsparingly, Loge observes the transformation of the Gods and describes the terrifying reality that has overcome them: without Freia's golden Apples, the Gods' youth and strength have faded, the tree branches have drooped, and decaying fruit has fallen to the ground. Loge is immune to their misery because he is only a half-God, one who does not need their delicate youth-preserving fruit. Loge gloats as he witnesses the Gods' dilemma and forecasts their impending doom,

Fricka reproaches Wotan as the cause of the Gods' horrible predicament, their present shame and disgrace. She rouses Wotan and prompts him to act with resolve. Wotan raises his Spear and announces his decision that the Gods will secure Freia's ransom. He bids Loge to join him to assault Nibelheim and seize Alberich's Gold. Cynically, Loge cruelly taunts Wotan, reminding him that his lofty purpose should be to rescue the Gold and return it to the Rhinemaidens, but Wotan contradicts him furiously, explaining that his sole purpose is to secure Freia's ransom. Loge continues to taunt Wotan with his sarcasm, suggesting that they descend to Nibelheim through the Rhine, but Wotan refuses, preferring to avoid meeting the lamenting Rhinemaidens.

As a sulphurous vapor rises, Wotan and Loge disappear into a fissure in the rocks and proceed to descend into the caverns of Nibelheim.

Scene 3: Nibelheim

In Nibelheim, the thunderous, frenzied, rhythmic sounds of hammering on anvils musically portray the enslaved Nibelung Dwarfs forging Gold for Alberich.

Hammering of the Nibelungs

The vapor recedes and reveals a dark, rocky, subterranean chasm. A red glow from the smith's fires illuminates Wotan and Loge as they enter Nibelheim.

Since Alberich seized the Rhinegold and fashioned the Ring, he has enslaved all the Nibelung Dwarfs, brutally forcing them to mine more gold and more treasure from the bowels of the earth.

Lament of the enslaved Nibelungs

The din of the hammering smiths rises to a loud crescendo and then gradually dies away. Alberich appears while dragging his shrieking brother Mime. To overcome his fears of being robbed of the Ring, Alberich commanded Mime, the most skilful of the Nibelung smiths, to mold a Tarnhelm, a magic helmet that can make anyone who wears it metamorphose into any shape or become invisible. Mime swears that he has been unsuccessful in molding the Tarnhelm. However, Alberich suspects that his brother has indeed fashioned the magic helmet, but is concealing it from him in the hope that he will use it himself to overcome his stronger brother. Alberich threatens Mime to produce the helmet by brutally beating and thrashing him. Mime makes stumbling excuses, admitting that the work is indeed finished but that he has been holding it back to see if it warrants improvement. In his fright he lets the delicate magic helmet fall. Alberich immediately seizes it, takes it in his hand, examines it critically, and delights in his discovery of the long-sought Tarnhelm.

Tarnhelm

Alberich places the Tarnhelm on his own head and tests its powers by invoking a spell: "Night and darkness - nowhere seen!" At once, to Mime's astonishment, Alberich disappears, leaving only a cloud of vapor appearing where he was standing. When Mime inquires about the whereabouts of his brother, the invisible Alberich proceeds to thrash him unmercifully.

Still only visible as a column of vapor, and even more confident of his powers, Alberich imperiously announces to the Nibelungs that they are his slaves forever, and viciously commands them to kneel before their master. He further admonishes them that they must dutifully tend to their work, because with his new magical powers he will be scrutinizing them in invisible form. Alberich roars, curses, whips the Nibelungs, and then disappears. The slaves begin their frenzied hammering amidst howls and shrieks. Mime groans, wails, and sinks to the ground in pain and terror.

When Wotan and Loge arrive, they discover the whimpering Mime and raise him to his feet. In answer to their inquiries, the Dwarf relates the history of the Nibelung's sad fate; that his brother Alberich forged a Ring from the ravished Rhinegold, and that with its power he has enslaved the entire Nibelung race, vanquishing their once innocent happiness in which they forged trinkets and toys for their womenfolk. Now, the brutal Alberich uses the Ring's magic power to locate the Gold, and then forces the Nibelungs to mine, melt, cast it into bars, and heap it into mounds. Mime reveals that he succeeded in making the Tarnhelm, but that he was unaware of the secret spell that could animate it. Mime reveals his despair; he is a fool who has been punished for his labors.

Mime's Despair

Wotan and Loge laugh at the grotesque and lamenting Mime. The Dwarf is bewildered and inquires as to their identity. Wotan and Loge assure him that they are friends who have come to liberate the Nibelungs. Suddenly, Alberich is heard approaching. Mime runs about wildly in helpless terror and urges the strangers to be on their guard.

Wotan seats himself while Loge remains by his side. Alberich enters briskly from the inner caverns, now transformed back to his own shape, and with the Tarnhelm hanging from his side. He whips a throng of frightened Nibelungs who are laden with metalwork that they pile up in a huge mound. Then, he orders them to return to the mines and dig for more gold. He draws the Ring from his finger, mutters a mysterious incantation, and immediately the shrieking Dwarfs, including Mime, scatter and flee from him in terror.

Servitude

Alberich halts suspiciously before the two strangers. He brandishes the Ring threateningly at them, admonishing them to tremble in terror before the great lord of the Ring.

Warily and distrustfully, Alberich scans the intruders and inquires the reason for their presence in Nibelheim. Wotan replies that they have heard about his great achievements and power and have come to witness them. With cajolery, Loge reminds Alberich of their earlier friendship; after all, he is none other than the fire-God who has brought comforting warmth to the Dwarf's sunless cave, and brought fire for his forges. Alberich refuses to be duped, recalling that the duplicitous Loge once pretended to be his friend, but now consorts with the "light-elves" who dwell above. (*Lichtalben,* the light-elves; Alberich himself is a *Schwarzalb*, a black-elf.) Alberich reveals that he no longer fears Loge because his power now rests in his Hoard; what they see is trivial, for day by day his Hoard grows and increases his glory and power.

Wotan inquires what value his wealth provides in the caves of Nibelheim where the Hoard can buy him nothing. Alberich boasts that his treasure provides the power to bend the whole world to his will; he will transform the Gods into his vassals, and those who live, laugh and love on earth, will be deprived of happiness. He boasts that he has renounced love, and at his command all humanity shall renounce love because they will yearn for wealth and power: Alberich's Ring and the great Hoard he has amassed through its powers. And those despicable, deceitful Gods who dwell in bliss in majestic Valhalla must beware, for their power will crumble before the might of the Nibelung's Ring and Hoard; and all women who once despised the ugly Dwarf will yearn to satisfy him.

The Hoard

Alberich has revealed his inner soul: he is the incarnation of hatred and evil Will, a destructive yet powerful force that Gods and men will have to reckon with. Alberich's contemptuous laughter provokes Wotan's outrage, but Loge intervenes to restrain the Godhead, and advises him to control his anger. Loge proceeds to placate Alberich with his usual smooth assurances. He compliments Alberich's wonderful achievements that have provided him with limitless power, and have forced all the Nibelungs to kneel before him.

With deferential care, Loge hints that Alberich should be cautious not to let his envious Nibelungs revolt and destroy him. He suggests that while the Ring remains in Alberich's possession his power is secure, but he would be vanquished if a thief stole the Ring from him while he slept. Loge cunningly appeals to Alberich's vanity, and the evil Dwarf falls into his trap. Alberich replies arrogantly that he has cleverly foreseen danger and has protected himself with the Tarnhelm, a magic helmet which can change his shape or make him invisible at will.

Urged on by the cunning Loge, Alberich's magically endowed Tarnhelm will become his undoing. With pretended awe, Loge compliments Alberich's Tarnhelm as perhaps the greatest marvel of the universe, an additional implement to insure his eternal might and power. Loge coaxes Alberich's egotism by goading him to demonstrate his ingenious wonder. The vain Dwarf becomes willing and eager to prove his wizardry, and asks Loge what shape he would like him to assume. Loge makes no choice, casually telling him that the deed confirms the word. Alberich obliges, places the Tarnhelm on his head, and murmurs a spell: "Dragon dread, turn and wind." Instantly, Alberich disappears; in his place, a huge serpent writhes on the ground, stretching its gaping jaws towards Wotan and Loge.

The Serpent

Loge pretends to be paralyzed with terror and pleads for mercy; Wotan breaks into hearty laughter and ironically compliments Alberich on his wondrous magic. The serpent vanishes and Alberich reappears in his own form, eagerly seeking their praise for his spectacular feat. Loge assures him that he has proven himself, and that they can no longer be skeptics about his magic powers. Loge again feigns admiration for Alberich and then cunningly invites him to perform a smaller transformation, advising the Dwarf that in a smaller size he could more easily escape potential danger.

Vainly, Alberich agrees to accommodate Loge's request, but inquires how small he wants him to become. Loge replies that he should become small enough to creep into a toad's crevice. Alberich, reveling in the simplicity of the request, murmurs his spell once again, and in his place a toad appears. At a quick word from Loge, Wotan immobilizes the toad with his foot, and Loge takes it by the head and seizes the Tarnhelm. Instantly, Alberich becomes visible, transformed back to his own shape and form.

Alberich curses them while struggling helplessly. Loge binds him with a rope. They drag the bound Alberich to the shaft from which they entered Nibelheim, and the three of them disappear.

Scene 4: The mountain heights

Wotan and Loge ascend from Nibelheim with their captured victim. Alberich furiously belittles himself for his foolishness and blind trust, and admits that he has learned his lesson; he will be wiser and less disingenuous in the future. Loge goads him sarcastically, gleefully dancing about the captive Dwarf and provoking Alberich to curse and vow revenge against the rogue and robber. Alberich demands his freedom, which Loge promises him after Alberich surrenders all the Nibelung's treasure.

Alberich, in an aside, comforts himself by reasoning that if he can save the Ring he can recreate the Hoard. He announces that he will summon the Hoard for them if they will untie his hand. As Loge frees his right hand, the Dwarf places the Ring to his lips and murmurs a secret command that summons the Nibelungs, who emerge from the clefts and begin to amass the Hoard. Alberich, ashamed and disgraced by his bondage, hides his face as he imperiously orders his enslaved Nibelungs to be quick with their work and not look upon him. He again kisses his Ring and holds it out commandingly, causing the terrorized Nibelungs to flee back into the clefts.

After the Hoard is amassed, Alberich demands his release and asks for the Tarnhelm to be returned to him, but Loge bluntly advises him that it must remain with them. Alberich curses him, but consoles himself with the knowledge that he can again force Mime to make another Tarnhelm.

Wotan then demands Alberich's Ring. Alberich cries out in desperation, offering his life but not the Ring. Wotan becomes insistent and asks Alberich how he came to possess the Ring, and where he found the Gold to fashion the Ring, all the while knowing the truth about his theft. Alberich suddenly has a revelation and realizes that his captors are the duplicitous Gods; intuitively he realizes that their intentions are to steal his Ring that will secure their power. He weighs the moral scales between himself and the Gods and reasons that both share a common purpose; he concludes that the Gods themselves would have stolen the Gold from the Rhine had they known how to forge the Ring from it.

On the scale of morality Wotan and Alberich are in perfect balance. Nevertheless, Wotan cannot withdraw because he is irrevocably committed to his course of wrongdoing, caught in a net of his own weaving in which he is yet unable to foresee the horrifying consequences of his actions.

Wotan wants the all-powerful Ring, and ruthlessly flings himself on the Dwarf and tears it from his finger. The God, like Alberich, has become possessed with the power inherent in the Ring. He places the Ring on his finger, contemplates it, and revels that it now belongs to him; with the all-powerful Ring, he now is the incontestable ruler of the world.

Alberich, with a horrible shriek, laments his ruin, prompting Wotan to give Loge permission to release the impotent Dwarf. Loge dutifully unties Alberich and tells him he is free to leave. Alberich greets his freedom with a wild and contemptuous laugh, and then condemns his assailants by invoking a horrifying Curse on the Ring.

Curse on the Ring

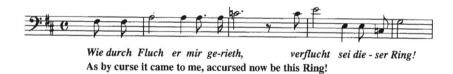

Wie durch Fluch er mir ge-rieth,   *verflucht sei die - ser Ring!*
As by curse it came to me, accursed now be this Ring!

Alberich's Curse condemns any possessor of the Ring; that each possessor of the Ring shall become consumed with torment, misfortune, harm, anxiety, and death. And those who do not possess the Ring, it shall be destroyed by envy.

Torment and Misfortune

With a demoniacal laugh, Alberich disappears into the clefts. Cynically, Loge asks Wotan if he heard the Dwarf's fond farewell. Wotan disregards Alberich's Curse, his thoughts totally consumed by the power inherent in the Ring that he now possesses.

The Giants return with Freia, followed by Fricka, Froh and Donner. Fricka rushes to Wotan and anxiously asks him for news about his mission into Nibelheim. Wotan points to the Hoard and assures her that by force and guile the Gods were victorious, and that Freia's ransom has been secured. With Freia's return, the Gods' youthful freshness is restored.

Wotan offers the Giants the Nibelung Hoard as payment for Freia's freedom. At first, Fasolt becomes reluctant, saddened at the thought of relinquishing Freia, but then decides that if he must lose her he wants the treasure heaped so high that it will hide her from his sight. The two Giants thrust their staves in the ground on either side of Freia to measure the Hoard they want amassed for them. Wotan, sick with a sense of shame and degradation, bids that they proceed quickly. The Giants heap up the Hoard between two staves, assisted by Loge and Froh,while Fafner, in his frenzied greed, searches for crevices, and packs the pile more tightly so that more Gold can be amassed.

Wotan turns away in profound disgust, commenting that he feels disgraced. Fricka adds to his torment by reproaching him for his ambitious folly of building Valhalla. As Fafner cries out for more Gold, Donner circles about him furiously, threatening the greedy Giant with his hammer. Loge assures the Giants that they have the entire Hoard, but when Fafner peers more closely at the dense pile he is able to see Freia's golden hair through an opening. He immediately demands that the Tarnhelm be thrown in to fill the void. Wotan, ever more disgusted, reluctantly orders Loge to add the Tarnhelm to the pile to fill the crevice.

Fasolt, still grieving that Freia will no longer be his prize, peers more closely at the heap and laments that there still exists a gap through which he can see Freia's shining eyes. Loge protests that it cannot be filled because the Hoard is quite exhausted, but Fafner points to the Ring on Wotan's finger and demands that it be used to plug the gap. Loge assures Fafner that Wotan intends to return the Ring to the Rhinemaidens from whom the Gold was ravished, but Wotan contradicts him, swearing adamantly that he will not yield the Ring to anyone. Loge protests that Wotan has reneged on his original promise to return the Ring to the Rhinemaidens. Wotan defends his decision to keep the Ring, denying that he is bound by any promises made to Loge, and then turns to Fafner and urges him to make a substitute request.

Fasolt angrily pulls Freia from behind the pile. He accuses the Gods of reneging on their promise, and as such, they have forfeited Freia forever. Fasolt begins to leave, but Fafner holds him back. Fricka, Donner, and Froh appeal to Wotan to relent, but he has become intransigent, too overcome by the idea of possessing the Ring and its power. He again proclaims that he will not yield the Ring, and turns away from them in blind, furious anger, remaining impervious both to the Giants who threaten to abduct Freia, and the pleas of the other Gods.

The present crisis of the Gods can only be resolved by the intervention of a world force greater than even the Godhead Wotan himself. Darkness suddenly descends and a bluish light appears from a rocky cleft: Erda, the Goddess of earth and wisdom, becomes visible as she rises from below the ground to half her height. Erda is the mother of the

Norns who weave threads that prophesy the world's destiny. She is a prophetess whose wisdom provides her with the knowledge of the past and the future of the universe. Erda cautions Wotan and advises him to return the Ring to the Rhinemaidens:

Erda, Goddess of wisdom

The Gods stand in awe and become speechless. Erda stretches out her hand commandingly to Wotan, again bidding that he relinquish the Ring to evade the Curse pronounced on it. Erda, the woman who possesses the entire world's wisdom, confounds Wotan by prophesying the downfall of the Gods even if he does not return the Ring: "All that exists must come to an end. A day of gloom dawns for the Gods: again I charge you to give up the Ring!"

Downfall of the Gods

Wotan responds thoughtfully to Erda's grave, mysterious and enigmatic pronouncement. As he moves desperately toward her to learn more, the bluish light fades. As she slowly disappears she utters a final message to the confounded God: "I have warned you; you have learned enough; brood now with care and with fear." Wotan turns to anxiety as he ponders thoughtfully and profoundly on Erda's last words.

Fearful, Wotan decides to heed Erda's advice. He becomes overcome by a bold sense of resolution, turns to the Giants while brandishing his Spear, and then hurls the Ring upon the Hoard. Freia, now rescued, runs to the Gods who embrace her in relief.

As Fafner begins to pack the Hoard into an enormous sack, the Giants begin to quarrel over their treasure. Fasolt demands equal share of the Hoard, but Fafner reminds his brother that he became foolish and lovesick over Freia, and had to be convinced to exchange her for the Hoard. Besides, if Fasolt had won Freia, would he have shared her with him? As such, Fafner justifies the greater part of the Hoard for himself.

Fasolt appeals to the Gods for justice, but Wotan contemptuously turns his back on him. Sarcastically, Loge counsels Fasolt to surrender the treasure, but be sure to take the Ring.

Fasolt assaults Fafner and insists that the Ring belongs to him as compensation for Freia. The Giants struggle for the Ring, each seizing it in turn. Finally, Fafner knocks Fasolt to the ground with a blow from his staff, and then wrenches the Ring from his dying brother's hand. The first materialization of Alberich's curse becomes realized. After Fafner places the Ring on his own finger, he proceeds to quietly pack the remainder of the Hoard. The Gods stand in horrified silence, astonished that Alberich's Curse has struck so quickly. Fafner completes the packing of the entire Hoard and departs with the great sack on his back.

Cynically, Loge congratulates Wotan on his incomparable good fortune: he had great luck when he seized the Ring from Alberich, but he has greater fortune now that he has ceded it, for the all-powerful Ring and its Curse will bring misery and death.

Fricka approaches Wotan cajolingly, asking him why he does not enter the noble fortress that awaits him, but Wotan is overcome by a profound sense of guilt, fully realizing that he freed Freia by acquiring her ransom through evil and deceitful actions. Wotan fears the consequences of his actions and resolves that he must soon consult Erda for her wisdom.

Donner ascends a high rock and swings his hammer against it to invoke the elements.

Donner: The Hammer

He - da!   He-da! He-do!   Zu mir, du Ge - düft!
Heda! Heda! Hedo! To me all you mists and vapors disperse!

Donner's crashing hammer evokes a blinding flash of lightning that bursts from the clouds, followed by a violent thunderclap. In the gleaming sunlight a great rainbow appears, extending as a bridge from the mountain top for the Gods to enter Valhalla.

Rainbow Bridge

The Gods gaze admiringly at the awesome sight of their new fortress. All proceed toward the rainbow bridge except Loge, who cynically and nonchalantly comments that the Gods are hastening toward their doom; he is ashamed of their deceit and duplicity, and no longer wants to share their activities. He prefers to remain behind and transform himself once more into an elemental and wayward flickering fire.

From the depths of the Rhine valley below, the haunting voices of the Rhinemaidens are heard. Their poignant laments call for the return of their Gold and disturb Wotan, who inquires whose plaints he hears. Loge tells him that the children of the Rhine are lamenting their stolen Gold, provoking Wotan to curse them for annoying him in his moment of glory. Loge calls down to the Rhine and delivers the message that it is not Wotan's Will to recover their Gold, but rather, that they should share in this moment of the Godhead's glory. As Wotan begins to pass over the bridge, the Rhinemaidens break into a more poignant lament, condemning those on earth as false and contemptible.

The Gods cross the rainbow bridge and gloriously enter their new fortress, seemingly confident that their power will remain secure, and with no thought of the inevitable consequences of their failure of conscience. Freia has been rescued, but the all-powerful Ring, Hoard, and Tarnhelm are now in Fafner's possession, jeopardizing the peace of the world.

Wotan knows that he himself cannot wrest the Hoard from Fafner, because that would represent a fatal violation of the Laws etched on his Spear. His thoughts become preoccupied with the idea of creating a surrogate who will act on behalf of the Gods, a hero independent of the Gods' Will, who will rescue the treasures from Fafner.

Wotan's thoughts then turn to creating a powerful Sword, a divine weapon that will possess magical powers, a Sword that will arm a future hero who will defeat Fafner, recapture the Ring and the treasures, and return the Ring to its primal innocence in the waters of the Rhine, thereby redeeming the world from its present evil by purifying the Ring from Alberich's Curse.

Sword

The Valkyrie

("Die Walküre")

Music drama in three acts

Music composed by Richard Wagner

Drama written by Richard Wagner

Premiere: Hoftheater in Munich, 1870

The Valkyrie **is the second music drama of**
The Ring of the Nibelung **("Der Ring des Nibelungen")**

Principal Characters in The Valkyrie

Siegmund, a Volsung ("Wälsung"), mortal son of Wotan	Tenor
Sieglinde, Siegmund's twin sister	Soprano
Hunding, a Neiding tribesman, Sieglinde's husband	Bass
Brünnhilde, a Valkyrie, daughter of Wotan and Erda	Soprano
Wotan, Godhead	Bass
Fricka, Wotan's wife, Goddess of marriage	Mezzo-soprano
The Valkyrie sisters: Gerhilde, Helmwige, Waltraute, Schwertleite, Ortlinde, Siegrune, Grimgerde, Rossweisse	Sopranos

Synopsis of events

About 20 years have passed since the events of *The Rhinegold.* During this time, the Ring, Tarnhelm and Hoard have been in the possession of Fafner, the Giant. Fafner used the Tarnhelm to transform himself into a ferocious Dragon in order to protect the treasure that he guards in a forest cave at Neidhöhle.

Wotan is haunted by the possibility that Alberich's Curse will be fulfilled; that Fafner will be defeated by the evil Alberich, who will recover the Ring and use its powers to annihilate the Gods and enslave the world.

As the Gods entered their new Valhalla fortress at the end of *The Rhinegold,* Wotan envisioned a subterfuge to resolve his political and moral dilemma, a way in which to recapture the Ring and purify it from Alberich's Curse; his strategy was to sire a mortal hero, a surrogate acting on his own free Will and independent of the Will of the Gods, who would recapture the Ring and redeem the world from its evil Curse.

After Wotan sired the Volsungs, the twins Sieglinde and Siegmund, with a mortal woman, he lived in the forest with his son Siegmund, and trained the future hero for arduous combat. He placed an invincible Sword in an ash-tree for the young hero to find in his greatest need. At the same time, Wotan reinforced Valhalla's defenses against invasion by the Nibelheim Dwarfs by siring the Valkyries, nine valiant warrior daughters who gathered slain heroes from the battlefields, and revived them to protect the Gods and Valhalla.

In Act I of *The Valkyrie*, after Wotan's son, Siegmund, finds his long-lost twin sister, Sieglinde, they fall in love with each other. Siegmund seizes the divine Sword Nothung and rescues Sieglinde from her oppressive husband, Hunding, Siegmund's Neiding enemy. Siegmund and Sieglinde escape to consummate their holy, incestuous union.

In Act II, Wotan's wife, Fricka, invokes the high moral principles that the Gods represent, and convinces Wotan that neither he nor his favorite Valkyrie daughter, Brünnhilde, should interfere in the forthcoming battle between Siegmund and Hunding. But during the combat, Brünnhilde defies Wotan's command and intervenes on Siegmund's behalf, not only because she believes that she has acted according to Wotan's subconscious Will, but also because she has become emotionally stirred by the love between Siegmund and Sieglinde.

In Act III, Wotan punishes Brünnhilde for her disobedience; he removes her Godhood, and places her in an eternal sleep encircled by fire, a barrier so fierce that it can only be penetrated by the greatest of mortal heroes.

Story Narrative with Music Highlights

Act I: The interior of Hunding's forest dwelling, in which there is a large ash-tree.

A ferocious storm rages, and the musical imagery depicts the crash of thunder, lightning, and the furious swirling of wind and rain.

The Storm

As the storm subsides, Siegmund stumbles into an unknown dwelling to seek refuge. He has been wounded in battle and in a frenzied state of fear and terror because he is being pursued by his enemies. He stands immobile and guarded before the great entrance door at the rear of the dwelling, his hand remaining on the door latch as he looks around warily. His clothes are disheveled, and he is exhausted and frightened, pained in both body and spirit. He sees no one, and assures himself that he is safe from his pursuers. He enters, closes the door, and staggers toward the hearth, where he falls exhausted on the bearskin rug.

Siegmund's Fatigue

Sieglinde enters from another room, imagining that the sounds she heard were those of her husband, Hunding, returning from the hunt. She becomes startled when she notices the stranger stretched-out out before the hearth. She bends over his body to determine if he breathes, and is suddenly overcome by an incomprehensible wave of tenderness and pity for the stranger.

Sieglinde's Tenderness

Sieglinde fills a drinking horn with water and offers it to the awakening stranger. He drinks it heartily and expresses his deep gratitude. As he gazes at her, he subconsciously recognizes her and senses that a mysterious bond exists between them; her kindness and sympathy arouse deep emotions within him, and console his pain and weariness.

Dawning of Love

After Siegmund inquires about his whereabouts, Sieglinde advises the stranger that he is in Hunding's home, and that she is his wife. She urges him to rest until her husband's return. Apprehensively, Siegmund expresses his hope that her husband will not deny hospitality to a wounded and weaponless man.

Siegmund explains that his life has been burdened by distress and the agony of continuing warfare; his shield and spear were just shattered in battle. He fled his enemies, but they continue to pursue him.

Sieglinde momentarily leaves the stranger, and then returns with a horn filled with mead. She offers it to him eagerly, but he refuses to taste it until her lips have first touched it. Afterwards, he drinks the mead and gazes at her warmly, sensing a stirring of his emotions that transcends gratitude. He lowers his gaze gloomily, and exclaims in a trembling voice that she has provided solace to an ill-fated man.

Siegmund describes himself as "Woeful," because misfortune pursues him wherever he goes. Thus, he declares that he is fearful to remain, because he would surely bring unhappiness to Hunding's home.

Volsung's Misfortune

Siegmund starts to leave, but Sieglinde dissuades him, crying out impulsively that he should remain. She declares with unrestrained emotion that he cannot bring ill fate where it already resides. Her revelation causes Siegmund to stare at her searchingly; she lowers her eyes apologetically, trying to hide her feelings of shame and sadness. Deeply moved by her apparent unhappiness, he decides to remain. They stare at each other sympathetically, each inwardly expressing the most profound inner emotions of desire and yearning.

Suddenly, ominous horns announce the approach of Hunding, who is heard outside leading his horse to the stable.

Hunding

Hunding appears at the door in full hunting regalia, armed with shield and spear. He pauses at the threshold, visibly confounded by the sight of a stranger in his house. Immediately, he turns to Sieglinde with a look of stern inquisitiveness. Sieglinde explains that she found the stranger on their hearth, faint and weary, and that she tended to him as a guest. Sensitive to the sudden tension, Siegmund defends her, claiming that the woman should not be reproached for offering a stranger rest and drink.

Hunding replies that his hearth and home are sacred to strangers in need. He removes his armor and hands it to Sieglinde, who hangs it on the branches of the ash-tree. Hunding gruffly orders his wife to prepare the meal, and Sieglinde obediently fetches food and drink from the adjacent room. While she prepares the table, she compulsively and involuntarily keeps her eyes fixed on the stranger. Hunding becomes suspicious of their glances at each other, and even more skeptical when he compares their features, commenting to himself that they not only look alike, but that the stranger, like his wife, has a serpent's mark in his eyes. (A hereditary characteristic of the Volsung race: Wotan's children.)

Hunding tries to conceal his agitation and inquires how the stranger found his dwelling. He continues by asking the stranger his name. Siegmund becomes fearful, reluctant to reveal himself to Hunding. Sieglinde notices Siegmund's agitation, and expresses visible sympathy and tenderness as she also awaits his response. Siegmund's hesitation further provokes Hunding's suspicion, causing him to boldly suggest that the stranger could not deny an answer to his wife. Dutifully, but initially embarrassed, Sieglinde asks the stranger his name.

Siegmund begins the grave story about his conflicted past, a life that has been exposed to torturous sorrow and pain; he explains that his life has not been "Friedmund" (Peaceful) nor "Frohwalt" (Joyful), but rather "Wehwalt" (Woeful). He explains that he knew his father as Wolfé, a strong warrior. One day, he and his father returned from the hunt and found their dwelling turned to ashes by the Neidings: his mother was dead, and his twin sister had vanished. Afterwards, he and his father lived in the woods and were continuously hunted by their enemies. Hunding interjects that he knew neither Wolfé nor his son, but heard of their reputation as great warriors.

Siegmund recounts that one day he and his father were furiously assaulted by the Neidings. During the onslaught, he was separated from his father, who subsequently vanished. Afterwards, he left the forest to live among men and women, but he found only mistrust, wrath, and animosity: he sought happiness in the world but found only grief; indeed, misfortune follows in his wake, and his life has been truly "Wehwalt" (Woeful). Sieglinde indicates a warm empathy toward the stranger's tortured life, but Hunding interprets his sad fate as the Will of the Norns, the weavers of human destiny who obviously had little love for him.

Sieglinde inquires why the stranger is now weaponless and seeking refuge. Siegmund explains that he rescued a distressed maiden because her brutal kinsmen were seeking to force her into a loveless marriage. He fought and killed her brothers, but then the maiden died as she grieved over the bodies of her dead kinsmen. Afterwards, the surviving kinsmen assaulted him and shattered his spear and shield. He fled and they pursued him, wounded and weaponless.

Siegmund turns earnestly toward Sieglinde, confident that she understands the fate of a man who is unable to live in peace. Sieglinde appears to be deeply moved by the stranger's story, her subconscious thoughts becoming strangely engrossed in her own Volsung past.

Volsungs

Hunding rises brusquely, unable to suppress his anger. As a Neiding tribesman, Hunding realizes that he has returned home to find his hated enemy in his own dwelling. He must honor the tradition of providing sanctuary for a stranger, but this same man has killed his kinsmen. In revenge, Hunding challenges Siegmund to mortal combat in the morning. Sieglinde tries to pacify the two enemies, but Hunding gruffly orders her away. Sieglinde stands motionless while overcome with pity and compassion for the stranger.

Sieglinde's Pity and Compassion

Before she leaves, she opens the cupboard and shakes spices into a drinking horn that she prepares for Hunding. As she begins to depart to an inner chamber, she looks toward Siegmund with intense yearning. Then she directs her eyes toward the ash-tree in which the divine Sword is buried; Siegmund carefully follows her glance, although he is unaware of its meaning. Hunding rouses himself from his somber brooding and proceeds to retire. As he removes his weapons from the branches of the ash-tree, he gruffly reminds Siegmund to prepare himself for combat until death.

Alone, Siegmund becomes melancholy and despairing as he contemplates his impending battle with Hunding. He recalls his father's unfulfilled promise, that in his most desperate need, he would find an all-powerful Sword. Yet, he now finds himself weaponless in an enemy's house, vulnerable to Hunding's hateful vengeance. Siegmund's thoughts become frenzied, and he cries out for his father Wälse, who seems to have abandoned him.

Wälse!

SIEGMUND

Wäl - se!   *Wäl - se!*   *Wo*   *ist dein Schwert?*   *Das starke Schwert,*
Wälse! Wälse! Where is your sword? The trusty sword,

"Wälse! Wälse! Where is your Sword? The trusty Sword!" Suddenly, a flicker of fire from the hearth illuminates the ash-tree, causing Siegmund to notice the faint yet partially visible hilt of a Sword.

Sword

The hearth fire extinguishes and leaves the room almost totally dark. Sieglinde returns, and advances lightly and rapidly toward Siegmund. She tells him that Hunding is asleep because she drugged his drink, but that more importantly, Siegmund must flee from mortal danger. She tells him that he could protect himself with the mighty Sword that is imbedded in the ash-tree; if he can retrieve it, he is truly the noblest and strongest of heroes.

Sieglinde explains the mystery of the Sword's presence. After she was sold to Hunding as his wife, she was overcome with sorrow and shame. A stranger suddenly appeared before her, an old man dressed in gray, who wore a large hat so low that it hid one of his eyes, while his one visible eye gleamed with menace and terror. Strangely, while in his presence, she was fearless and felt consoled from her sorrow. The stranger heaved a great Sword into the trunk of the ash-tree, announcing that it will belong only to the man who possesses the heroic power to withdraw it from the tree. All tried in vain to remove the Sword from the tree, but Sieglinde reveals that she intuitively knows that it is he, the stranger, who is the true hero who can accomplish the deed.

Sieglinde expresses her hope that one day she may find that friend who will comfort her, relieve her sufferings, and end the shame and disgrace that have befallen her. Siegmund embraces her compassionately, and with intense emotion tells her that he is both her friend and rescuer. He will not only win the Sword from the tree, but he will win her as his bride; both have shared suffering, but now they will share the joy of love.

Friendship

SIEGLINDE

O   fänd   ich ihn heut'   und   hier,   den Freund,
Oh might I find that friend here today,

Suddenly, the large rear doors open to reveal a beautiful spring night, the full moon's radiance flooding the newfound lovers. Siegmund compulsively draws Sieglinde closer to him with ardent tenderness.

"Winterstürme"

SIEGMUND

Winterstürme wichen dem Wonnemond,   in mildem Lichte leuchtet der Lenz;
Winterstorms of May have waned, and Spring sparkles in gentle radiance;

Siegmund and Sieglinde celebrate nature's blessing of spring: the storms of winter have transformed into the beauty of May, and birds sing while flowers bloom. As Siegmund embraces Sieglinde, he proclaims that their love lured the spring; Sieglinde proclaims that this spring provides the warmth for which she had longed through her lonely and friendless icebound winter. She admits that from the moment her eyes met his, she yearned for him: he has restored hope to her dark soul.

Sieglinde's Bliss

SIEGLINDE

O   lass   in   Nä - he   zu dir   mich nei - gen
Oh let me hold you yet closer to me,

das hell   ich schau-e   den   heh   -   ren Schein,
and see more brightly your noble countenance.

Siegmund and Sieglinde recognize their common ancestry; as Volsungs; they are Wälse's children. Sieglinde solemnly proclaims the name of her lover and rescuer: Siegmund, "Victorious Protector and Guardian."

Siegmund springs toward the ash-tree, seizes the Sword, and invokes its power. Siegmund's pronouncement is accompanied by Alberich's Renunciation of Love motive; nevertheless, Siegmund is not renouncing love, but announcing the rebirth of love. Siegmund names the weapon Nothung ("Needful"), the Sword that shall serve him in his most desperate need.

Nothung! ("Needful!")

SIEGMUND

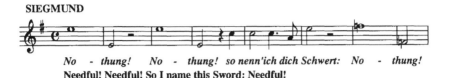

No - thung!   No - thung! so nenn'ich dich Schwert: No - thung!
Needful! Needful! So I name this Sword: Needful!

Siegmund wields the Sword before the astonished and ecstatic Sieglinde. He announces that by extracting the Sword from the ash-tree, he has won her as his bride; and the Sword shall be his bridal gift to her. Together they shall flee from sorrow and celebrate the bliss of their love. Sieglinde responds with equal rapturous passion. They fall into each other's arms, and Siegmund ecstatically claims his bride: "Bride and sister, I am to be your husband and brother; so that the Volsungs will flourish!" Siegmund and Sieglinde escape into the night to consummate their sacred union.

Act II- Scene 1: A mountain pass, a gorge in the background, and a high rocky ridge.

The energetic musical imagery portrays Wotan's warrior daughters, the Valkyries, riding through the skies bearing slain heroes to Valhalla.

Wotan, dutifully bearing his sacred Law-laden Spear, heralds the arrival of his favorite Valkyrie daughter, Brünnhilde. He immediately alerts her that she has much work to perform for the Gods; soon there will be combat between Siegmund and Hunding, and Brünnhilde must aid Siegmund in the battle. Elated by the news, Brünnhilde energetically expresses her joy: "Hojotoho! Heiaha!"

"Hojotoho!"

BRÜNNHILDE

Ho - jo - to -ho!   Ho - jo - to -ho!   Heia - ha!   Heia-ha!

Brünnhilde looks down into the valley and alerts Wotan that Fricka is approaching in her ram-drawn chariot, whipping the terrified beasts with a frenzied urgency. Brünnhilde, not wanting to intercede in her father's domestic disputes, disappears, leaving Wotan alone to face his angry wife.

Fricka appears and immediately erupts into moral outrage and indignation. She invokes social propriety and the sanctity of marriage, reminding her husband that she is the sacred guardian of holy wedlock. As such, she has vowed to punish the Volsung pair who have betrayed and mocked Hunding by consummating an incestuous and illicit union. Therefore, she must heed Hunding's cries for vengeance.

Wotan tries to placate his wife, suggesting that the Volsung twins have done no harm, but have merely surrendered to the magic of love. Fricka finds her husband's approval of their incestuous union unacceptable; she rebuffs him furiously and urges that he punish them. Contrarily, Wotan frankly suggests that they bless the new bond of love, an exalted substitute for the loveless marriage of Sieglinde and Hunding.

Wotan's casual attitude toward marriage further provokes Fricka's indignation. She reminds him that he dishonored the morality of the Gods by betraying their own marriage; during his wanton escapades he sired the Volsung twins and the eight Valkyrie daughters with mortal women, and then Brünnhilde with Erda, the Goddess of Wisdom.

"O was klag'ich um Ehe und Eid"

FRICKA

O   was klag'ich um Ehe und Eid,   da zuerst du selbst sie versehrt.
Oh why do I weep for wedlock and vows, which you are the first to profane.

Fricka, now a humiliated and inexorably jealous woman, becomes more impassioned as Wotan's uneasiness intensifies. He defends the Volsungs as the Gods' surrogates. After all, his sole purpose was to sire Siegmund so that he would become an independent hero who would redeem the Gods. Fricka enlightens Wotan that his subterfuge was a blatant violation of the Gods' sacred Laws. As such, she orders Wotan to cease to protect Siegmund, and withdraw the magic spell on Siegmund's Sword.

Wotan reacts angrily, but then restrains himself. Fricka perceives that he is weakening and uneasy, and she grows more confident and aggressive. She again admonishes him that Siegmund must be punished because Wotan has mocked and scorned Fricka's Laws of sacred marriage.

Fricka demands that Wotan renounce Siegmund and leave his destiny to fate; that he withdraw the magic spell on the Sword and promise that the Valkyrie, Brünnhilde, will not intervene in the forthcoming combat between Siegmund and Hunding. Wotan is impotent against Fricka's moral rectitude. If he complies with Fricka's demands, all of his hopes to recover the Hoard and abolish Alberich's Curse will be shattered. He makes a final passionate plea to her, but the unmerciful Fricka remains intransigent and implacable. Wotan, bound by Law, reluctantly agrees to abandon his son, the ill-fated hero Siegmund.

"Deiner ew'gen Gattin heilige Ehre beschirme heut' ihr Schild!"

FRICKA

Deiner   ew' - gen Gattin   hei- lige Eh - re   beschir - me heut'ihr Schild!
Guard your eternal consort's shield today!

Wotan is in a moral dilemma, trapped in a web of his own weaving, and bound by the very forces that empower him. He stole the Gold from Alberich by force and deceit, and knows that another immoral act would compound his crimes and signal his downfall. Wotan is ambivalent and paradoxical: he is a God, but he is also morally flawed, and his predicament urges him to break out of his prison of faults and return to the lofty state of directing human evolution and progress toward a higher world order.

Brünnhilde now returns and senses that a grave confrontation has just taken place. As Fricka prepares to depart, she majestically orders Wotan to vindicate the honor of the Gods, reminding him that he must order Brünnhilde to refrain from protecting Siegmund. Utterly defeated and dejected, Wotan mutters, "Take my oath!"

Wotan's' Dejection

Fricka, triumphant in her moral victory, departs haughtily.

Brünnhilde gazes at her dejected father with dismay. He seems haggard and despairing, his soul tortured by profound conflicts. Mournfully, Wotan explains his tragic conflict to Brünnhilde, "I am bound by my own shackles, the least free of all those that live!" He vents his shame and distress: "I am the saddest of all living!" He admits that as his youthful passions vanished, his soul grew thirsty for power and he wanted to rule the world; he protected himself with binding Laws. Brünnhilde sinks at his feet and lovingly implores him to confide in her, the truest of his children, and the Will of his inner soul.

Wotan reviews the past events that took place in *The Rhinegold,* and ominously predicts that his lust for power will signal the downfall of the Gods. His intentions were noble when he engaged the Giants to build Valhalla, a fortress from which he would bring peace and order to the world, and foster humanity by raising moral consciousness. The Nibelung Alberich renounced love and stole the Rhinemaiden's Gold, from which he fashioned the all-powerful Ring and magic Tarnhelm. Wotan admits that he allowed himself to be cunningly lured by Loge to steal the Nibelung's treasures as a substitute payment to the Giants instead of Freia. After he discovered the Ring's immeasurable power, he wanted to keep it for himself. He admits that he had participated in fraud and deception; in the end, he gradually surrendered to evil, and he had become as immoral as those he fought to transform.

Erda, the Goddess of wisdom, counseled him to return the Ring to the Rhinemaidens, warning him that it would doom the Gods if he retained it. But she refused to tell him more, and in fear, he ceded the Ring to the Giant Fafner as part of the payment for Freia. He sought Erda for more advice, and in union with Erda, he sired his beloved daughter Brünnhilde, his alter ego.

The evil Alberich forever lurks in the shadows, tormented by rage and envy, and unceasingly schemes to steal the Ring from Fafner. Fafner, transformed into a ferocious Dragon by the Tarnhelm, now sleeps on the treasure. As long as it remains in his protection, the Gods and the world are secure. But if Alberich should wrest the treasure from Fafner, it would spell the Gods' doom. Alberich now has bought a woman's love, and in her womb lies the Nibelung's fruit of hate and envy; Alberich, like Wotan, has also sired a surrogate son who will seek to recapture the Ring and use the Ring's power to enslave the world and doom the Gods.

Need of the Gods

Since the Gods are bound by their own laws, Wotan sired Siegmund, his surrogate who would recapture the Ring, restore it to the Rhinemaidens, and purify it of its Curse. But Fricka pierced through his deceitful subterfuge, and overwhelmed him with shame; now, he is honor-bound to yield to the moral force of her demands and withdraw his protection of Siegmund. It is as if Alberich's Curse pursues him everywhere; his hopes that Siegmund would succeed have vanished, and he must abandon and betray his beloved son.

Wotan regretfully concedes that all of his efforts have been in vain; he is tired of struggling, and has turned to despair. Fricka has intervened and invoked the sanctity of binding law that has impeded his involvement in recovering the Ring. With resignation, he invokes the downfall of the Gods: "Once I craved for power, but now I curse the work I have begun! I leave Valhalla and all its pomp to the greedy Nibelungs! There is only one fate that I await – my downfall!"

Wotan tells Brünnhilde that they must obey Fricka's command, and that in the fight between Siegmund and Hunding, they must betray Siegmund and he must fall. Brünnhilde protests and tries to persuade him to alter his brutal decree, even vowing that she will never fight against the hero whom Wotan loves. But he warns Brünnhilde that if she fails to heed his command, she will provoke his implacable wrath and become subjected to appalling punishment: "Siegmund is to die; this must be the work of the Valkyrie!"

Wotan rushes away in frustration and despair. Brünnhilde remains terrified and bewildered, saddened by her father's distress.

Act II - Scene 2: Sieglinde and Siegmund in flight

Brünnhilde catches sight of Siegmund and Sieglinde approaching the mountaintop. She watches them for a moment, sighs mournfully that she must betray the young Volsung hero, and then disappears into a cave.

Sieglinde is exhausted and terrified by the horn calls she hears from the pursuing Hunding, imagining that his bloodhounds have surrounded them, have ravaged Siegmund's flesh with their fangs, and have splintered his Sword. Siegmund gently and lovingly calms her agitation.

Suddenly, Sieglinde hears Hunding's booming horn calls again and flees from Siegmund in panic and terror, hysterically urging him to leave her because she has brought him only misfortune. Sieglinde's guilt has transformed her rapturous love into self-loathing, because she is convinced that she has brought scorn and shame to the brother and friend who has rescued her. Siegmund assures her that he will avenge the shame she feels by killing Hunding with Nothung, the divine Sword.

With a last cry of "Brother! My brother! Siegmund!", the trembling Sieglinde collapses. Siegmund bends over her anxiously, kisses her brow tenderly, and seats himself so that her head rests on his lap while she is sleeping.

Act II - Scene 3: Brünnhilde and Siegmund

Complete darkness envelops the mountaintop. In a sudden burst of moonlight, Brünnhilde is seen emerging from the cave. She strides slowly and solemnly towards the Volsungs, and then pauses to contemplate the man whose fate rests in her hands. The Valkyrie's solemn thoughts are about Wotan's command to abandon Siegmund, a duty that for the first time has left her confused and perplexed.

Fate or Destiny

Brünnhilde stands earnestly as she stares at Siegmund, the Volsung who will soon die and join Wotan's brave and faithful heroes in Valhalla.

Brünnhilde addresses Siegmund by name and tells him that she has come to summon him to Valhalla. Since his death is imminent because his Sword no longer possesses its magical powers, he will join the hallowed fallen heroes who surround Wotan in Valhalla. There, he will find his father, Wälse, and smiling wish-maidens, however, Sieglinde is fated to remain on earth. At these words, Siegmund bends gently over Sieglinde, kisses her softly, and then turns in agitation to the Valkyrie: "Then greet Valhalla for me, greet Wotan for me, greet Wälse for me, and all the heroes: also greet the gracious wish-maidens. I will not follow you! Rather I will destroy Sieglinde and myself!"

Brünnhilde warns Siegmund that he will fall to Hunding, but Siegmund scornfully contradicts her and announces that it is Hunding who will die; she should take Hunding to her majestic Valhalla. Gently and solemnly, Brünnhilde urges Siegmund to heed her calling, advising him that his Sword's magic spell has been withdrawn and it will fail him.

Announcement of Death

Siegmund bends tenderly over Sieglinde, laments his cruel fate, and in an outburst of humiliation, condemns his traitorous father, Wälse, cursing him for allowing his son to be slain by his enemy. Siegmund proclaims that if he must die, he would prefer to go to Hella's underworld rather than to Valhalla; let his death bring anguish and grief to his father's pitiless heart.

After Brünnhilde promises to protect Sieglinde after he is gone, he replies that he alone will protect Sieglinde. In his agony, he raises his Sword and threatens to kill Sieglinde and himself. Brünnhilde becomes suddenly transformed by Siegmund's profound love for Sieglinde. For the first time, she senses that love is more worthy of protection that all the Gold and power in the world, profound human sensibilities that were unimaginable to the Valkyrie before.

Brünnhilde erupts into a sudden outburst of emotion and declares that Sieglinde shall live, and that Siegmund shall not be parted from Sieglinde. Brünnhilde has decided to disobey Wotan and defend Siegmund; she will intercede on his behalf and he will triumph in his fight against Hunding.

As the sound of Hunding's ominous horn is heard in the distance, Brünnhilde tells Siegmund to raise his Sword without fear, because the Valkyrie will restore the Sword's magic and will assure his victory. As Brünnhilde disappears, Siegmund looks after her with joy and relief.

Heavy thunderclouds descend, darken, and envelop the mountaintop. Siegmund bends tenderly over the sleeping Sieglinde, vowing that when the fight is over, peace will end her pain. He leaves her alone as the sound of Hunding's horn draws nearer. With his Sword drawn, he climbs the mountain resolutely, and then disappears into the darkness.

Sieglinde stirs restlessly in her nightmarish slumber, overcome with horrible memories of her childhood, her wedding and those harsh and hateful strangers, and the flames that destroyed her Volsung home. She calls out for her mother, and then her brother: "Siegmund! Where are you?"

Roars of thunder and blinding flashes of lightning awaken Sieglinde. She leaps up, gazes around in terror, hears the sound of Hunding's horn approaching, and then hears Hunding's hoarse voice urging his enemy to meet him in battle. Siegmund is heard asking where his enemy hides, and boasts that he will make a mockery of him. He exclaims with pride that he is no longer weaponless, because he has drawn the great Sword from the ash-tree.

Suddenly, the two men are visible at the summit of the mountain, locked in ferocious combat. Hysterically, Sieglinde cries despairingly that the mad Hunding should slay her first, but a flash of lightning makes her reel back as if blinded. Brünnhilde intervenes in the battle, sheltering Siegmund and guarding him with her shield. But just as Siegmund is about to aim a fatal blow at Hunding, a red glow breaks through the clouds and Wotan appears, thundering that all should stand back. Wotan holds his Spear before Siegmund's Sword, and angrily shouts to Siegmund to draw back because his Spear will splinter his Sword. Brünnhilde shrinks back in terror as the weight of Wotan's Spear shatters Siegmund's Sword. At once, Hunding thrusts his spear into Siegmund's breast and kills him.

Brünnhilde rushes to Sieglinde, who has heard Siegmund's death sigh and has fallen almost lifeless to the ground. Brünnhilde gathers the fragments of Siegmund's splintered Sword, raises Sieglinde on her horse, and disappears with her. When the clouds divide, Hunding is seen with his spear buried into the breast of the dead Siegmund. Wotan, leaning on his Spear, gazes with infinite sadness at the fallen hero's body. Now that he has obeyed Fricka, Wotan is free to execute his Will. Overcome with grief at his betrayal of his son Siegmund, he scornfully and bitterly exclaims to Hunding: "Get away, slave! Kneel before Fricka and tell her that Wotan's Spear has upheld her honor. Go! Go!" With a contemptuous wave of his hand, Wotan strikes Hunding dead.

As silence descends on the mountaintop, Wotan suddenly remembers that Brünnhilde repudiated his Will. He erupts into uncontrollable rage, shouts that Brünnhilde has disobeyed him, and that she will pay dearly for her transgression. Amid thunder and lightning, and with fury and purpose, Wotan disappears in pursuit of his daughter, determined to punish her for disobeying his wishes and Will.

Act III: A wild landscape at the summit of a rocky mountain

The fierce Valkyrie maidens rendezvous from their various battlefield expeditions before returning to Valhalla. With slain heroes across their saddles, they ride through the skies, stridently shouting their Hojotoho's, and then descend on the rocky summit.

Ride of Valkyries

Gerhilde, Ortlinde, Waltraute, and Schwertleite, have assembled on the mountaintop and greet each other joyously. Before riding off to Valhalla together, they hesitate. They realize that Brünnhilde is absent, and watch anxiously for her arrival.

Suddenly, the Valkyries see Brünnhilde in the distance, and are astonished that a woman lies across her saddle. After Brünnhilde descends, she breathlessly appeals for her sisters' aid, telling them that Wotan pursues her because she disobeyed him by protecting Siegmund and rescuing Sieglinde. She pleads for a swift horse to replace her exhausted charger so she can escape from her father's wrath. Ortlinde and Waltraute cite a thundercloud approaching from the north, and announce that Wotan is approaching, relentlessly and furiously driving his steed towards the mountaintop. Fearing Wotan, the terrified Valkyrie sisters refuse to lend Brünnhilde a horse.

Sieglinde, devastated by the death of Siegmund, reproaches Brünnhilde for protecting her; she wants to die as well, and implores Brünnhilde to strike her sword through her heart. But Brünnhilde exhorts her to cling to life, for she bears Siegmund's child. Brünnhilde's prophecy transforms Sieglinde from despair into fervent exaltation, and she cries out ecstatically.

"O hehrstes Wunder!"

As clouds roll in and thunder roars, the terrified Valkyries urge Brünnhilde to flee with Sieglinde, but Brünnhilde decides to remain to face the angry Wotan. She urges Sieglinde to leave and tells her that she will find safety in the vast eastern forest where Fafner, transformed into a huge Dragon, lies in a cave guarding the Hoard. Although the forest is perilous and dangerous for a woman, Brünnhilde tells Sieglinde to be brave and defiant, endure hunger, thirst and hardship; because she bears the world's bravest of heroes in her womb. Brünnhilde gives Sieglinde the fragments of Siegmund's Sword and urges her to preserve them for her child, who one day shall forge the splinters anew; his name shall be "Siegfried" ("He who shall rejoice in victory.")

Sieglinde quickly takes the shattered Sword fragments and responds ecstatically with a great cry of thankfulness and gratitude.

As the storm increases in violence, the enraged voice of Wotan is heard calling his disobedient daughter to face him. Brünnhilde appeals to her sisters to shield her from Wotan's wrath, and they draw themselves together and conceal her in their midst. Wotan arrives and strides furiously towards the Valkyrie sisters and threateningly demands to know the whereabouts of Brünnhilde. With agitated cries, the Valkyries try to appease his wrath, but he scolds them for their display of womanish weakness. He announces that Brünnhilde scornfully broke their holy bond by defiantly disobeying his wishes and Will. With unrelenting force, he summons Brünnhilde to come forward and receive her punishment.

Humbly, but with firm steps, Brünnhilde emerges from amidst the protection of her Valkyrie sisters. She pauses a short distance from the Godhead and stoically addresses him: "Here I stand father, pronounce your punishment."

Wotan scolds her for betraying him; his treasured Valkyrie whom he created to revive heroes for Valhalla, now has provoked a hero against the Gods. With anger and heartbreak, he announces that Brünnhilde has willed her own punishment; that she will no longer seek fallen warriors for Valhalla.

Brünnhilde's Destiny

Wotan

Nicht weis' ich dir mehr Hel - den zur Wal; nicht führst du mehr Sieger in meinen Saal;
You will no longer seek warriors, no longer bring heroes to fill my hall;

She will also be stripped of her godly powers; she will be an outcast, banished forever from her father's sight. Sadly, Brünnhilde questions why he must take away all that he has given her, but the implacable Wotan reminds her that she defied him; as such, he decrees that she must remain on the mountaintop, defenseless in sleep. Brünnhilde sinks to the ground, half-kneels before Wotan, and implores him to relent. Meanwhile, Wotan turns savagely and harshly to the wailing Valkyries and orders them to leave or else they will share their sister's fateful punishment. The Valkyries shriek wildly and then ride away.

Brünnhilde kneels before Wotan in despair and utter dishonor. She timidly but poignantly asks her father if her deed was in truth as shameful and disgraceful as to merit such a severe punishment. She asks him to look into her eyes and silence his rage, master his anger, and expose his hidden guilt in betraying his favorite child.

Brünnhilde protests that in protecting Siegmund she was merely executing her father's deepest inner wishes. When he announced his supreme sacrifice to placate Fricka, she pierced beneath his words and knew exactly what lay in his heart; that in his soul he desired Siegmund's victory. Indeed, she presumed to substitute her wisdom for his, because she knew that he wanted Siegmund to live, and she felt that she was performing the highest form of obedience to her father's subconscious Will.

Brünnhilde continues to defend her actions, and describes how she became consumed with emotion and compassion for Siegmund's love for Sieglinde. She began to pity and love him, and suddenly recognized that the love that was filling her heart was no different than Wotan's love for his Volsung son.

Love for the Volsungs

Wotan recognizes that Brünnhilde believed she was fulfilling her father's Will, the Will he was forbidden by Law to enact. Indeed, in the end her actions preserved the Volsungs from destruction by saving Sieglinde and her unborn child. Nevertheless, Brünnhilde's betrayal has broken their holy bonds and she must be punished.

Brünnhilde, transformed into a mortal, will remain in a deep sleep, bound and weaponless, until she becomes rescued by the first man who shall find and awaken her. Brünnhilde erupts into passionate protest, begging Wotan to surround her with such fiercely flaming terror that only the bravest and greatest of heroes would be able to rescue her.

Sleep

Wotan's anger slowly dissolves. He raises Brünnhilde to her feet, gazes into her eyes, and bids and emotional farewell to his favorite daughter.

Farewell

"Muss ich dich meiden"

Wotan places a kiss on Brünnhilde's eyes and embraces her tenderly, savoring his love for his daughter for the last time. As Brünnhilde sinks into his arms, unconsciousness gently overcomes her. Wotan leads her gently to a low bank underneath a tree, lays her down, closes her helmet, and covers her completely with the great Valkyrie shield. He moves slowly away, and then turns around once more, staring at her sorrowfully.

With solemn decision he points his Spear towards a large rock and strikes it three times, summoning Loge to encircle her with fire. At once, flames fiercely and furiously rise, a spectacular bridal fire that will strike fear into the heart of all but the boldest of men. Wotan proclaims: "For one alone can win the bride, one freer than I, the God!" Prophetically, Wotan's thoughts turn to Siegfried, Sieglinde's unborn child.

Siegfried: the future hero

   Wotan stretches out his Spear, as if imposing a spell, and pronounces his final invocation to the future hero who will win Brünnhilde: "He who does not fear the sharpness of my Spear-point shall pierce through this fierce-flaming fire!"

   As Wotan departs, he looks back with sorrow and deep resignation in the direction of his beloved daughter, Brünnhilde.

Siegfried

Music drama in three acts

Music composed by Richard Wagner

Drama written by Richard Wagner

Premiere: Bayreuth Festspielhaus, 1876

Siegfried is the third music drama of
The Ring of the Nibelung ("Der Ring des Nibelungen")

Principal Characters in Siegfried

Siegfried, son of Siegmund and Sieglinde	Tenor
Mime, a smith, brother of Alberich	Tenor
Brünnhilde, a Valkyrie, daughter of Wotan and Erda	Soprano
The Wanderer (Wotan, the Godhead)	Bass-baritone
Fafner, the Giant, transformed into a Dragon	Bass
Alberich, a smith brother of Mime	Baritone
Erda, Goddess of wisdom	Contralto
The Woodbird	Soprano

Background of Siegfried

About seventeen years have passed since the events of *The Valkyrie.* Brünnhilde remains in sleep, encircled by a fiercely flaming fire. After *The Rhinegold,* the Nibelung Dwarf Mime, wanting to escape from his brother Alberich's abuse, left the caverns of Nibelheim and established his forge in the forest near Neidhöhle in the vicinity of Fafner, who guards his treasure in a cave. Fafner, the Giant, used the Tarnhelm to transform himself into a Dragon in order to protect his Hoard, Ring, and Tarnhelm.

After Siegmund was slain, Sieglinde, his twin sister and bride, pregnant and in possession of the shattered fragments of the Sword, was led to Mime's cave. The Dwarf provided her with food and shelter and helped her give birth to her son Siegfried; Sieglinde died during childbirth.

Mime raised Siegfried as his own son, but kept him ignorant of his background and the world. He nurtured the young Siegfried's strength so that he would become a fearless hero, a surrogate who would kill Fafner and capture the Hoard for Mime himself.

(In *Siegfried,* Wagner departed from his Nibelung mythological sources and addressed the archetypal conflict of the young boy learning fear; he adapted many of the elements from Grimm's early 19th century fairy tale, "The Story of a Youth Who Went Forth to Learn What Fear Was.")

Siegfried begins in the darkness of Mime's cave and ends in the brilliance of the sky, symbolically the hero's transformation to maturity, consciousness and awareness, which is cultivated and developed through the powerful love between Brünnhilde and Siegfried.

The maturing Siegfried is an uninhibited man of nature, the idealized noble savage unencumbered and uncorrupted by the trappings of civilization. Emotionally, Siegfried is an impetuous child who displays a combination of admirable as well as objectionable characteristics: he is a lonely, gentle and sensitive boy who is psychologically maturing and desperately yearning for companionship and maternal love. But in his pursuit of understanding the incomprehensible world surrounding him, he can become deeply troubled at times confused and frustrated, as well as uncertain and insecure.

Mime has preposterously taught Siegfried that he is both his father and mother, but by learning about life in the forest, Siegfried realizes that Mime lied to him. Mime's inferior features are repulsive to Siegfried, who has seen his own image reflected in a stream, and noted their physical differences. Nevertheless, the young Siegfried is trapped in Mime's world, and at this time, the malevolent Dwarf represents his only road to wisdom, knowledge, and eventual freedom.

Siegfried displays an exuberant love of life and freedom, an eagerness for adventure and a profound sense of purpose and resolution. Yet his boisterous adolescence and youthful vitality can erupt into impetuous explosions of nastiness and sadism; he terrifies the weaker Mime by bringing a bear into the cave, gloating with pleasure as Mime shakes in fear.

Mime is by no means a kindly old Dwarf, but rather, a treacherous, despicable, murderous villain, who has fostered Siegfried for the sole purpose of slaying the Dragon and seizing the Ring and Hoard for himself; he has unabashedly planned to murder Siegfried after the young surrogate accomplishes the deed.

Wagner described his conception of Mime in his stage directions: "He is small and bent, somewhat deformed and bobbling. His head is abnormally large, his face a dark ashen color and wrinkled, his eyes small and piercing, with red rims, his gray beard long and scrubby, his head bald and covered with a red cap. He wears a dark gray smock with a broad belt about his loins: feet bare, with thick coarse soles underneath. There *must be nothing approaching caricature in all this:* his aspect, when he is quiet, must simply be eerie; it is only in moments of extreme excitement that he becomes outwardly ludicrous, but never too uncouth. His voice is husky and harsh; but this again ought of itself never to provoke the listener to laughter."

Mime is the incarnation of evil and villainy, demented by his monomania to capture the treasure and acquire its powers. Night and day Mime seethes with revenge against his cruel brother, Alberich, and dreams of the day when he will gain the Ring, enslave the Nibelungs, and master the world. Mime has nurtured Siegfried's strength and vitality and intentionally failed to teach him fear. But to slay the Dragon, the young hero needs an omnipotent sword; Mime, an expert blacksmith, has been unable to forge a sword for him.

In Act I, Wotan appears in Mime's cave disguised as the Wanderer; he wear a long cloak and a large hat covers one eye. He challenges Mime to a game of wits, ultimately predicting that only a fearless man will be able to temper the hardy fragments of the impregnable Sword: Nothung.

Siegfried desperately wants to learn fear, and Mime assures him that he will learn fear when he confronts the terrifying Dragon. In anticipation of his forthcoming combat with the Dragon, Siegfried himself reforges the fragments of Nothung, while ironically, Mime observes while he intrigues to kill the boy after he has accomplished the deed.

In Act II, Wotan, again disguised as the Wanderer, encounters Alberich and plants the seeds of his brother Mime's betrayal; he alerts Alberich that Mime plans to recover the entire treasure for himself by poisoning Siegfried after the young hero has slain the Dragon and recaptured the Hoard, Ring and Tarnhelm.

Mime brings Siegfried to Fafner's forest cave. Siegfried awakens Fafner and fearlessly slays him with his Sword Nothung. After tasting the Dragon's blood, Siegfried is able to understand a forest bird that advises him to claim Fafner's treasure, beware of Mime who plots to kill him, and rescue the maiden who is encircled by fire on a nearby mountain. Taking the bird's advice, Siegfried ignores the Hoard as valueless, but seizes the Ring and Tarnhelm.

The taste of the Dragon's blood also enables Siegfried to understand Mime's thoughts. When Mime offers Siegfried a poisoned drink, Siegfried is aware of Mime's villainous intentions and immediately slays him. With the bird as his guide, Siegfried begins his journey to the mountaintop where Brünnhilde is sleeping.

In Act III, Wotan summons Erda to predict the destiny of the Gods; she predicts their imminent downfall. Wotan's hopes for the world's redemption now turn to the omniscient Brünnhilde and the young hero, Siegfried.

As Siegfried nears Brünnhilde's mountaintop, Wotan, still disguised as the Wanderer, confronts the impassioned hero. When the stranger tries to block his path with his Spear, Siegfried explodes into anger and smashes it to pieces with Nothung. Wotan erupts into indescribable emotional turmoil, realizing that his shattered Spear symbolizes the inevitable doom of the Gods.

Siegfried scales the heights of Brünnhilde's mountain, and then heroically passes through its flaming barrier. He awakens the sleeping Brünnhilde; his emotions have become so stirred that he has finally learned fear. Brünnhilde solemnly greets the sunlight. Brünnhilde is now a defenseless mortal woman and she surrenders herself to Siegfried's love; as such, she has likewise learned fear.

With feverish excitement, Brünnhilde and Siegfried share the ecstasy of their newfound love for each other. As the unwitting surrogate of Wotan, Brünnhilde will endow Siegfried with her wisdom and love, and nurture the young hero so that he will redeem the world and purify the Ring of its Curse. As such, the evil forces in the world will be defeated, and a new world order of noble ideals and elevated conscience will come into existence: "let the twilight of the Gods begin."

Story Narrative with Music Highlights

Prelude

The prelude to *Siegfried* presents a musical portrait of Mime's inner thoughts, his ceaseless monomania to gain possession of the Ring in order to become master of the world.

Mime's Thoughts and Reflections

The Hoard

Act I: In Mime's cave, there is a smith's forge, an anvil, and smith's implements. A flue ascends from the forge.

In his cave in the vast eastern forest of Neidhöhle, Fafner, metamorphosed by the Tarnhelm into a huge Dragon, is guarding the Hoard, Ring and Tarnhelm. Mime agonizes, frustrated because he is physically too weak and too impotent to slay the monstrous Dragon himself. To slay the Dragon also requires the forging of a far greater weapon than he has ever fashioned. He has tried to reforge the shattered fragments of Nothing, but lacks the skill; after each attempt, Siegfried easily shattered his work. With frenzied despair, Mime plunges himself once more into his work, all the while preoccupied with thoughts of how he can slay the Dragon and steal the Hoard, Ring, and Tarnhelm.

The Dragon

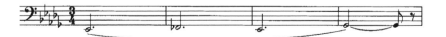

After Siegfried's horn call is heard from the forest, he enters the cave, restive and impetuous.

Young Siegfried

Siegfried has arrived with a tethered bear, and with wanton adolescence, directs the animal against the frightened Mime. Terrified, Mime shelters himself behind the forge. After Siegfried frees the bear to the forest, the trembling Mime emerges from behind the forge and rebukes the boy's bold impudence.

Siegfried erupts into scornful laughter, explaining that he hoped the bear would become a more compatible friend than the wretched Dwarf. In reality, Siegfried indeed intended to frighten Mime with the bear, hoping that it would force Mime to forge a sword that he had promised him. Mime shows Siegfried a sword he has been forging and hands it to him, all the while praising its sharpness. Siegfried slides his hand over the blade and fails to find its steel hard and true; he downgrades the sword, rejects it as a useless toy, and then strikes it on the anvil, breaking it into splinters. He then terrifies Mime by exploding into a rage, all the while castigating the Dwarf for boasting that he makes weapons of might, while in reality, all he forges is easily breakable rubbish. After Siegfried calms down, Mime complains that he can never seem to please the boy. He reproaches Siegfried as inconsiderate, ungracious, and unappreciative of all the unselfish kindness and indulgence that he has showered upon him.

Siegfried's Ingratitude

MIME

Als   zul - len - des   Kind   zog   ich   dich   auf,
I brought you up from a whimpering baby,

Mime's reprimand causes Siegfried to sulk and turn his back to Mime. Then Mime shows Siegfried the dinner he prepared, but Siegfried rashly knocks the meat and bowl from his hands. Mime reproaches him again, deploring the boy's lack of appreciation, and his failure to reward Mime for his love and devotion.

Mime reminds Siegfried that because of his irrepressible love for him he has devoted his entire life to rearing him, unselfishly providing him with clothes, food, a soft bed, many toys, and a ringing horn. Besides, he has also provided him with wise advice, knowledge and insight; while Siegfried roamed the forest with complete abandon, Mime remained at home toiling for him. Mime has made great sacrifices for Siegfried, but his reward has only been excruciating torment; the Dwarf begins to sob, overcome with self-pity and anguish.

Siegfried turns to Mime, fixes his eyes searchingly on him, and then harshly denounces the Dwarf. He sarcastically concludes that Mime indeed has taught him much, but he failed to teach him what he most desired to learn: to endure the sight of Mime's ugliness and evil. Siegfried proceeds to taunt Mime, asking him why he loves all the creatures in the forest more than the ugly Dwarf. Mime reproaches Siegfried, admonishing him that he speaks not from his heart; that in truth, he indeed truly loves the unselfish old Mime.

Mime's Love

Siegfried has learned about life in the forest and has witnessed how mothers shower love on their offspring. He asks Mime how he came about without a mother. Mime becomes embarrassed but assures Siegfried that he is both his father and his mother in one. Siegfried refutes him, noting that in the forest the child resembles the parent. After all, he concludes, he has seen his own face in the reflection of the stream, and his features are far from those of the ugly Dwarf.

Siegfried becomes obsessed to learn of his origins. To persuade Mime to reveal his background, he brutally seizes him by the throat and half chokes him. Mime frees himself, lamenting again that he has been a fool to expect gratitude from such an insolent boy.

Nevertheless, Mime acquiesces to Siegfried's insistence. He admits that he is neither Siegfried's father nor mother. He tells Siegfried that long ago he found a woman weeping in the desolate forest; he brought her to his cave and gave her shelter. While giving birth to her son Siegfried, she died. Sadly, Siegfried expresses his remorse about his mother's death.

When Siegfried asks why he is called Siegfried, Mime replies simply that it was his mother's wish. At first Mime tells Siegfried that he never knew his mother's name, but after a renewed threat by Siegfried, he reveals that her name was Sieglinde. Mime never learned his father's name, only that he had died in combat. Once more Mime begins to whine, but Siegfried interrupts him to inquire what proof he has that Mime is telling him the truth.

Mime ponders for a while and then produces the fragments of a broken sword, and explains that they represent the pitiful pay he received for his kindness to the woman; they are the shattered fragments of the Sword which his father wielded in his fatal fight. Siegfried becomes excited and orders Mime to begin forging the sword immediately, threatening him if he fails to forge it properly. The Sword will become Siegfried's instrument for his freedom; his rightful weapon, and with it, he will leave Mime, the forest, and go into the world, never to return to the horrifying ugly Dwarf whom he has now learned is not his father.

"Aus dem Wald fort in die Welt zieh'n"

SIEGFRIED

Aus dem Wald fort   in die Welt zieh'n: nimmer kehr' ich zu - rück!
I will go out into the forest, and never return!

Siegfried rushes impetuously into the forest, exhilarated and ecstatic by the prospect of his freedom. Alone, Mime reflects, confused and terrified. He becomes prey to new anxieties that interfere with his nefarious monomania to capture the Hoard. Siegfried was to be his surrogate who would slay Fafner and win the treasure for him, but now the headstrong boy is shattering his plans by resolving to leave him. Mime seats himself by the forge and ponders his dilemma: first, he must find a way to forge the powerful sword for Siegfried to slay the Dragon; and second, he must find a way to lead Siegfried to the Dragon's cave. In agonized frustration, Mime collapses in despair.

Wotan, disguised as the Wanderer, enters slowly from the back of the cave. He is an ominous looking man who wears a long cloak and a large hat set low over one eye. He approaches Mime, gravely and solemnly.

The Wanderer (Wotan)

The Wanderer greets the cringing Nibelung Dwarf and courteously requests the traditional grace granted to a weary wayfarer. When Mime asks the stranger's identity, he introduces himself as the Wanderer, the recipient of gracious hospitality from good men with whom he exchanges his profound wisdom. He points his Spear at Mime and comments that few men are wise enough to know their own needs, and he therefore graciously offers them the benefits of his wealth of wisdom.

The Dwarf urges the ominous intruder to leave, protesting that he is sufficiently wise and needs no counsel from strangers. Undaunted, the Wanderer calmly seats himself and proposes a combat of wits, a challenge in which he will offer his head if he is unable to answer any question the Nibelung Dwarf may ask him.

Mime becomes distressed, pondering a way in which he can rid himself of what he regards as an intrusive spy. Nevertheless, he is confident of his own cunning and decides to accept the stranger's challenge: he will gamble his hearth against the Wanderer's head, and ask the stranger three questions to test his boastful and arrogant knowledge.

Mime asks the stranger if he can tell him what race dwells in the caverns of the earth. The Wanderer replies that it is the Nibelungs who dwell in Nibelheim, former slaves of Alberich who had overpowered them with his magic Ring.

After further reflection, Mime asks what race dwells on the surface of the earth. The Wanderer replies that it is the Giants who dwell in Riesenheim. Two of them, Fasolt and Fafner, fought over the Nibelung's Hoard. Fafner slew his brother Fasolt and now guards the treasure, transformed into a Dragon.

The Wanderer requests the Dwarf's third question. Mime, rather baffled by the stranger's omniscience, reflects deeply. He then asks what race dwells on the cloud-covered heights. The Wanderer replies that it is the Gods who dwell in their fortress Valhalla. The Godhead is Wotan, who made a Spear-shaft from a branch of the World-ash-tree and governs the world by virtue of the Laws he carved upon it. With his power, Wotan restrained the Giants and the Nibelung Dwarfs.

The Wanderer lets his Spear touch the ground. It evokes a rumble of thunder, causing Mime to shrink back in terror. The Wanderer then asks if he has answered the Dwarf's questions correctly. If so, can he therefore hold on to his head? Timidly yet ingratiatingly, Mime nods his assurance, and then exhorts the stranger to go on his way.

But the Wanderer remains. Instead, he reminds Mime of the rules of their wager. As such, it is now the Dwarf's turn to gamble his wisdom against his head. Petrified, Mime pulls his wits together, gains confidence, and prepares to answer the Wanderer's first question.

The Wanderer asks what race received Wotan's wrath, even though he loved it more than all others in the world. Mime confidently answers that it was the race of the Volsungs, whom Wotan loved and cherished, but was forced to punish. As Wälse, Wotan fathered the twins, Siegmund and Sieglinde, whose offspring is Siegfried, the noblest and strongest of all the Volsungs. The Wanderer compliments Mime on his knowledge.

The Wanderer then asks who was the wise Nibelung who raised Siegfried as his surrogate to fight Fafner; and by what sword Fafner will die. Mime ponders the question and finds the answer absurdly easy. He rubs his hands in glee and announces that it is Mime who has sheltered Siegfried, and that the Sword is Nothung, the weapon wielded by Siegmund in his fatal battle against Hunding, and was shattered by Wotan's Spear.

Mime, highly pleased with himself, asks the Wanderer if he has saved his head. The Wanderer laughs cynically, assuring him that nowhere on earth is there wisdom like that of Mime. The Wanderer compliments Mime, but interjects that since he is so wise as to raise this young hero for his own purposes, perhaps he is wise enough to answer the third question.

The Wanderer inquires by whose hand the mighty pieces of the Volsung sword will be remolded into Nothung. Mime erupts into wild terror and fear, screaming pathetically that he does not know. As the most skillful of smiths, Mime has been unable to hammer or melt those cursed fragments. In an outburst of despair he throws his tools about and cries deliriously: "Who can shape the Sword that baffles my skill? Who can achieve this marvel?"

Finally, the Wanderer provides Mime with his infinite wisdom; the answer to the question that was the real purpose of his visit to Mime. He boldly informs Mime that the fragments of the Sword Nothung can only be forged anew by one who knows no fear, but that Mime must beware that this fearless man will slay him. The Wanderer smiles cynically, and then disappears into the forest.

Mime, crushed and threatened, contemplates the Wanderer's enigmatic words with a renewed sense of fear and terror. The Wanderer has prophesied that the fearless Siegfried will indeed reforge Nothung, and subsequently, he will kill Mime. Mime's anxiety transforms into terrorizing hallucinations. He stares despairingly at the sunlit forest, now seemingly alive with menacing lights that flash, swirl, quiver and dart. He imagines the roars of monsters opening their jaws and seizing him as their prey. In fright he shrieks, "Fafner! Fafner!" Then the horrified Mime collapses.

Siegfried returns to the cave, searches for Mime, and finds him behind the anvil. Mime is hardly aware of Siegfried's presence; he is musing about his baffling dilemma, confounded and tormented by the Wanderer's prediction. Suddenly he is struck by an idea; by teaching Siegfried fear, Mime will make Siegfried vulnerable, and then he will be able to exercise power over him.

Mime immediately incepts his plan. He complains to Siegfried that he has been careless in educating him. Although he taught him about the evil and duplicity of the world, he never taught him fear. Siegfried inquires disingenuously, "What is fearing? Is it a craft?" Mime responds by asking Siegfried if he ever felt fear and fright in his soul when night fell in the forest. Siegfried affirms with assurance that his heart always beats soundly. Nevertheless, Mime's description of fear arouses the lad's curiosity. He concludes that fear must be the strangest of feelings: shivering, shuddering, trembling, burning and fainting. Excitedly, Siegfried exclaims that he yearns to learn fear.

Mime decides to teach Siegfried fear by taking him to Neidhöhle, the eastern forest where a monstrous Dragon devours men. Siegfried becomes delighted and impatiently urges Mime to forge a powerful sword for his adventure. Mime wails again, complaining that the task is beyond his talents, however, one who knows no fear can indeed achieve it. Siegfried immediately recognizes his calling. He pushes the whimpering Dwarf aside, strides to the hearth, and announces that he, the fearless one, will reforge the splinters of his father's Sword.

Siegfried piles a great heap of charcoal on the hearth, blows up the fire, places the fragments of the Sword in the vise, and begins to file them vigorously. Mime observes him, offers advice, but his counsel is contemptuously rejected.

Siegfried files the fragments, forms them into a crucible form, and places them on the forge. He continues to tug at the bellows and plunges the white-hot crucible into the water, all the while lustily praising it. While Siegfried forges the Sword, he watches Mime with suspicion. The Dwarf's thoughts seem to be ominous, but Siegfried is unaware that the Dwarf is preoccupied with his diabolical plan to kill Siegfried with a poisoned broth after he slays the Dragon.

"Nothung! Nothung! Neidliches Schwert"

SIEGFRIED

No - thung! No - thung! Neidliches Schwert! Was musstest du zerspringen?
Needful! Needful! Conquering sword! What blow has served to break you?

Mime excitedly shakes some herbs into a pot to cook the poisonous broth. When Siegfried inquires what he is doing, Mime evades him by praising the young boy's forging skill. He comments that the lad has put the master to shame; from now on, Siegfried will be the smith and Mime will be the cook.

After Siegfried extracts the glowing steel from the fire, he lays it on the anvil: he has succeeded in forging the all-powerful Sword. He takes it from the anvil, brandishes it, and again plunges it into the water, laughing boisterously at the sounds of its hissing. Mime leaps about in delight because Siegfried's success in forging the Sword forecasts his own triumph: Mime, the former slave of his despised brother Alberich, will soon acquire the Hoard, Ring and Tarnhelm and master the world; the Nibelungs and Gods will soon cringe before him.

Forging the Sword

With a final blow of his hammer Siegfried sets the rivets in the Sword's handle, and victoriously greets the all-powerful Sword.

Siegfried proudly addresses his masterwork: "Show the cowards how you can shine! Cut through the false heart, and strike at the knave!"

He raises the newly forged Nothung, and with a mighty blow shatters the anvil into pieces. Mime, who had been exulting in his own triumph, becomes frightened as he realizes that Siegfried's Sword could become the instrument of the young hero's freedom and wisdom.

Act II: a knoll in the forest at Neidhöhle before Fafner's cave

Fafner: the Dragon

It is night. Alberich is crouched outside Fafner's cave, convinced that soon he will repossess the Hoard and master the world. Suddenly he recoils, terrified when he recognizes the approaching Wotan in his Wanderer's disguise. The two enemies confront each other. The vengeful Alberich reproaches the God with venomous wrath, indicting him for violating the sacred Laws on his Spear because he used force and deceit to steal his Hoard, Ring and Tarnhelm. Alberich further denounces the God for breeding a hero-race as his surrogate to regain possession of the Ring.

Alberich taunts Wotan by suggesting that doom awaits him, the penalty and punishment for his deceit. He announces that when he, Alberich the Nibelung, recaptures the Ring, he will destroy Valhalla and master the world. But the Wanderer fails to be moved by Alberich's threat. With quiet composure, he tells Alberich that he has come to Neidhöhle not to challenge or act against him, but to witness forthcoming events.

Calmly, the Wanderer announces that the Ring's destined master will deal with its power in his own way. He claims that he no longer has interest in actively pursuing the treasure, for its recapture rests in the actions of a hero who knows nothing about the Godhead, but who unwittingly will serve the Will of the Gods.

The Future Hero

Alberich rejoices in victory, because without the Gods' interference, no obstacles block his diabolical obsession to recapture the Ring.

However, the Wanderer bears a warning for Alberich, and cautions him that his greedy brother Mime has motivated a young hero to slay Fafner. Alberich responds to the threat casually, confident that he can cope with his despised brother and the innocent young hero. The Wanderer continues his prophecy; that Fafner will fall, and that the two Nibelung brothers will vie for possession of the Ring.

The Wanderer approaches Fafner's cave and calls out to awaken the Dragon. Fafner's deep voice booms from the dark recesses of the cave and asks who awakened him from his sleep. With irony, the Wanderer replies that it is a friend who will allow him to live if he yields the treasures to him.

Alberich intervenes with urgency, advising Fafner that a hero will soon arrive to challenge him. Fafner replies casually that he welcomes the combat. The Wanderer and Alberich warn the Dragon that the brave hero possesses a mighty Sword. However, the hero only seeks the golden Ring; if Fafner merely yields the Ring, the hero will not fight him, and he can retain the Hoard. Fafner growls and then bellows that he will keep all of his possessions; then he yawns and asks to be left to sleep in peace.

The Wanderer had anticipated Fafner's resistance to ceding the Ring. He turns to Alberich and laughs heartily because they have failed to convince Fafner. Then he offers advice to Alberich: "All things go as they must: no minute part may be altered." Before departing, the Wanderer cautions Alberich again to beware of his brother Mime. As he disappears into the forest, Alberich gazes intently after him, cursing the God viciously, and predicting the Nibelung victory and the downfall of the Gods. Alberich then slips into a cleft in the rocks to hide as he awaits the hero with the mighty Sword, and his confrontation with Fafner.

As day dawns, Siegfried and the Dwarf Mime arrive at Neidhöhle. After recognizing Fafner's cave, Mime announces that they need go no further. Siegfried urges Mime to leave him, satisfied that he has come at last to a place where he will learn the meaning of fear. Mime assures him that if he does not learn fear here at Neidhöhle at this moment, there is no other time or place for him to learn it.

Mime intentionally provides a horrifying description of the grim and grisly Dragon: vast jaws that can kill him with one snap, poisonous saliva that can rot his bones and body, and a huge tail that can crunch his bones like glass. Siegfried remains undaunted and confident, and inquires if the monster has a heart. And, if it is in the same place as in men? Mime's assurance prompts Siegfried to announce that he has nothing to fear, for he will drive the powerful Sword Nothung straight into the Dragon's heart.

Mime again tries to arouse Siegfried's fright and panic by telling him that when he sees the Dragon his senses will weaken, his heart will beat madly, and the forest will spin all around him. Mime then hopes that Siegfried will thank him for leading him to Neidhöhle, and will realize that Mime has great love for him. Siegfried's hatred of Mime resurfaces, and he frankly asks himself when he will rid himself of this horrible creature, a man who professes to love him, but for whom he feels only loathing and hatred.

Before Mime leaves, he tells Siegfried to wait until the sun reaches its height, for at that time the monster will crawl from his cave to drink water from the stream. Siegfried amuses himself with a pleasing idea that would rid him of the miserable Dwarf; that the Dragon might devour Mime while he drinks at the stream. Ironically, Mime urges the boy to call on him should he need him. The thought repulses Siegfried, who drives the Dwarf away with a furious gesture. As Mime departs, he reveals his treacherous inner thoughts: "Fafner and Siegfried, Siegfried and Fafner, that each the other might slay!"

Slowly, the forest stirs with the sounds of morning life.

Forest Murmurs

Siegfried stretches himself out comfortably under a tree. Although he is lonely he is delighted by the departure of the loathsome old Dwarf, and fervently hopes that he will never see him again. After he learned that Mime was not his father, he became joyful, but wondered how his true father looked? Siegfried also begins to yearn for his mother, wishing he could learn more about what she was like; surely her eyes were soft and shining and tender like those of the deer. Were they perhaps even more beautiful? He knows she bore him in sorrow and wonders if all mothers must die so that their young may live. He sighs and then imagines his happiness if he could only see his mother.

While Siegfried is lost in reverie, the forest murmurs grow louder, and he becomes attracted by the song of a woodbird in the branches above him.

The Woodbird

He muses whether the bird is trying to tell him something about his mother, and remembers that the irritable old Dwarf told him that there was meaning in the songs of birds, if men could understand them. But how can he communicate with the birds? Suddenly he thinks about exchanging melodies with the bird. He runs to the spring, cuts a reed with his Sword, and hastily shapes it into an instrument. When the bird sings again, Siegfried makes an attempt to imitate it, but his clumsy reed either blows false notes or gives no sound at all. He becomes boyishly peevish at his failure and smiles to acknowledge that the little songbird is his superior.

He concludes that perhaps the slender reed was not a fitting instrument. Instead, he places his horn to his lips and blows a vigorous, sustained call on it. The forest begins to resonate, and suddenly he senses something stirring in the background. Siegfried's horn has awakened the Dragon Fafner, who now exits his cave, dragging his monstrous bulk up to the knoll where he rests the front part of his body. The Dragon emits a huge yawn that astonishes Siegfried, who watches the Dragon with boyish delight.

The Dragon asks the boy who awakened him? Siegfried answers: "One who wants to learn what fear is. Hopefully I will learn it from you, or else, you will be food for my Sword." Fafner opens his gaping jaws, shows his teeth, and roars cynically: "I came for a drink, and now I find food!"

Fafner's anger increases as Siegfried taunts him. With defiant roars, he challenges the boastful boy to engage him in combat. The Dragon drags the rest of his clumsy body up the knoll, spouts venom from his nostrils, and lashes at Siegfried with his tail. The Dragon raises the front part of his body to throw his weight on the boy; as he does this, he exposes his breast. Quickly and instinctively, Siegfried plunges his Sword into the Dragon's heart.

Fafner groans with pain, tries to raise himself, and then sinks to the ground. Siegfried withdraws his Sword and leaps beside him. In a weakening voice Fafner asks the lad who he is, and who had urged him to this murderous deed, knowing that his own childish mind could never have conceived such a diabolic act. Siegfried accuses the monster himself of provoking him to combat.

Fafner proceeds to tell Siegfried whom he has slain. He recounts the story about the brother Giants, Fafner and Fasolt, who long ago were paid by the Gods for building Valhalla with the Hoard, Ring and Tarnhelm. Then Fafner murdered his brother and used the Tarnhelm to transform himself into a Dragon to guard the Hoard; and that by slaying him, the last Giant has fallen. The dying Fafner offers Siegfried profound advice: "Heed this well, blossoming hero; the one who drove you blind to this deed also plots your death! Mark it well! Heed my word!"

Siegfried appeals to Fafner to learn more about his origins. The Dragon merely repeats Siegfried's name with a sigh, and then utters his final words: "The dead can give you no knowledge."

Fafner, in his death agony, rolls to one side. The Dragon's blood has burned Siegfried's hand. Instinctively, he places his fingers to his mouth to suck away the blood. As he does this, the song of the birds once more captures his attention. He senses that they seem to be speaking to him; by tasting the Dragon's blood their song has become intelligible to him. One of the birds says: "Now Siegfried has won the Nibelung Hoard: it lies awaiting him there in the cave. If he wins the Tarnhelm too it would serve him for wonderful deeds; but if he finds the Ring it would make him lord of the world!"

Siegfried thanks the bird for its counsel, and enters the cave in search of its treasures.

Mime suddenly returns. He looks around timidly, assures himself that Fafner is dead, and proceeds warily towards the cave. Simultaneously Alberich emerges from the clefts and rushes toward his brother to bar his way. Each of the Nibelung brothers seeks to claim the treasure.

They confront each other with questions, arguments, and accusations. Mime claims the Hoard as a reward for raising Siegfried to defeat Fafner; Alberich claims the treasure because he stole the Rhinegold and renounced love to learn how to invoke the Ring's magic power. Mime claims that he fashioned the magic Tarnhelm that served Alberich so well; Alberich claims that it was through his invocation of the Ring's power that Mime was endowed with the skill to make the Tarnhelm.

Mime weakens and suggests a compromise in which they would share the treasure: Alberich would keep the Ring, but he would take the Tarnhelm. Alberich laughs scornfully, swearing that he will never let the Tarnhelm pass into Mime's hands, because he fears that his brother would deceive him while he sleeps. Realizing that his arguments are futile, Mime screams in rage; now it seems that nothing, not even the smallest share of the treasure will be his. Nevertheless, Mime proclaims that Alberich shall have no share either, because he will summon Siegfried to wield his powerful Sword as revenge against his brother.

At that moment Siegfried, unaware of the presence of the Nibelung Dwarfs, emerges from the cave. To his astonishment, Mime notices that the young hero took nothing from the treasure, except the Tarnhelm. However, Alberich curses Siegfried after keenly noticing that he indeed seized the Ring. Mime adds to Alberich's consternation by announcing he will convince Siegfried to give him the Ring. To avoid confronting Siegfried at this moment, Mime runs into the forest; Alberich slips into a cleft while muttering confidently that soon the Ring will be returned to him.

Siegfried walks slowly from the cave and gazes curiously at the Tarnhelm and the Ring that he took on the advice of the woodbird; to him they seem like mere trinkets, and he has no idea of their value. Nevertheless, he is dismayed because these treasures have not brought him what he desired; he still has not learned the meaning of fear.

While he places the Ring on his finger and affixes the Tarnhelm to his side, the woodbird suddenly announces that Siegfried has won the Tarnhelm and Ring, and that he should not trust the treacherous Mime. The bird tells him that because he has tasted the Dragon's blood he also will be able to understand Mime's thoughts.

Siegfried acknowledges that he understands the woodbird's advice and warning.

Siegfried, now confident and self-assured, observes Mime returning to Neidhöhle. Mime is unaware that Siegfried, having tasted the Dragon's blood, can now understand the Dwarf's treacherous thoughts; as such, Siegfried will be able to understand Mime's intentions for malice and deception.

Mime praises Siegfried with gushing compliments for his heroic victory over Fafner. Siegfried complains that the Dragon did not teach him fear, but more importantly, that he is grieved because Mime urged him to commit evil acts and the Dwarf remains unpunished; he now hates Mime more than the slain Dragon. Mime remains undaunted and continues to shower Siegfried with flattery and affection, although he becomes uneasy by Siegfried's unfriendliness. Mime's only concern now is to kill Siegfried with poison and capture the treasure.

Mime again pleads for Siegfried's compassion and understanding for the sacrifices he made for his "son," and urges him to yield the treasure or else his life will be in jeopardy. Siegfried's casual demeanor agitates and angers him.

"Siegfried, mein Sohn"

MIME

Siegfried, mein Sohn,das siehst du wohl selbst, dein Leben musst du mir lassen.
Siegfried, my son, you will see for yourself that you need me.

Mime shows Siegfried the broth which he claims he lovingly prepared for the hero's refreshment after his combat with the Dragon. Since Mime's thoughts are now intelligible to Siegfried, he knows that the broth contains poison. Siegfried refuses to drink it, prompting Mime to remind him that in the past Siegfried never hesitated to take refreshment from him. When Siegfried asks what herb the broth contains, Mime assures him that if he tastes it he will soon sleep peacefully. Inwardly, Mime laughs, knowing that as soon as the boy is asleep, he will kill him. Siegfried, reading Mime's sinister thoughts, confronts the Dwarf for wanting to kill him. The unsuspecting Mime becomes confused and defends himself furiously, vehemently denying Siegfried's accusations.

Mime again coaxes Siegfried to drink his poison, thinking to himself that this will be Siegfried's last drink. Mime's villainous thoughts suddenly fill Siegfried with violent hatred for the treacherous, murderous Dwarf. He raises his Sword, and with one swift blow, slays Mime. In the background, Alberich is heard laughing mockingly; his horrifying Curse on the Ring has just claimed another victim.

Siegfried carries Mime's body to the entrance of the cave. He heaves it inside, and pronounces his epitaph for the hateful and wretched Dwarf; that he may now guard his long-sought Gold without fear of thieves. He then drags the Dragon's body to block the cave entrance and blesses the rivals for the Gold; in death they have been victorious in their quest.

Siegfried decides to rest under a tree to be sheltered and shaded from the sun's heat. He delights at the chatter of the birds in the branches above him who seem to be singing about love. As he laments his loneliness, he suddenly feels a yearning for love and friendship. His mother and father are dead, he has no brother or sister, and the one companion he did have was that treacherous old Dwarf who tried to kill him.

Siegfried's desire for love

Siegfried asks the woodbird to advise him where he can find a faithful friend. The bird announces that a friend awaits him; she is Brünnhilde, who is sleeping on a fire-encircled rock. He should awaken her and win her for his bride.

Siegfried springs up abruptly and impetuously, his heart suddenly aflame with passion and yearning. He asks the woodbird how he can pierce the flames to awaken this glorious bride, and he is told that only one who has never known fear can accomplish it. The fearless Siegfried becomes ecstatic; he failed to learn fear from the Dragon, and therefore he can pierce the flames and find a bride and friend.

Siegfried asks the bird to lead the way to his bride. The bird hovers above him, teases him for a while, and then sets its course for Brünnhilde's fire-encircled rock; Siegfried follows anxiously.

Act III - Scene 1: the foot of a mountain below Brünnhilde's rock

It is night. A storm rages, and there are flashes of lightning and roaring thunder. Wotan has become tortured by the events he precipitated, the outcome of which he is unable to control. He is overcome with anxiety about the future of the Gods, the Ring, and Siegfried. After leaving Alberich at Neidhöhle, he hastened to Erda, the prophetess and Goddess of wisdom, to again seek her advice.

Wotan awakens Erda from her interminable sleep. As a bluish light glows from a dark cavern, Erda rises slowly from the depths; her eyes, heavy with sleep, are covered with frost, and her hair and garments emit a shimmering light. She inquires whose magic power has interrupted her dreams and sleep.

Wotan announces that the Wanderer appears before her. He tells her that he has roamed the world in quest of wisdom, and now seeks it from the wisest of women; the Wala, or prophetess, who knows all that stirs and breathes on earth, in the waters, or in the air. Erda responds gravely, telling him that while she sleeps and dreams, her daughters, the Norns, spin all that she knows; he should seek them to learn his destiny.

The Wanderer desperately pleads for Erda's wisdom to interpret events already set into motion. Erda evades his pleas and tells him to go to their child Brünnhilde, who possesses Erda's wisdom and can predict the destiny of the world. Wotan informs her that Brünnhilde has been punished, deprived of her Godhood because she scorned Wotan's Will, and that she is now a mortal lying in a deep sleep, awaiting a hero who can pierce the flames, awaken her, and win her for his bride. Erda reproaches him for punishing Brünnhilde, a loving daughter who fulfilled his innermost wishes; he defends truth and right, but reigns with untruth.

Erda tries to dismiss him, but he remains, insisting that she reveal how the Gods can avoid their downfall.

Erda predicts that Wotan's hope for the world's redemption rests with Siegfried, the young Volsung who has won the Nibelung's Ring without the Godhead's counsel and intervention. Alberich's Curse has no power over the young hero, because he is free from envy and knows no fear. Siegfried will awaken Brünnhilde, Erda's child, who possesses her mother's wisdom, and through their love they shall inherit the earth and redeem the world.

Destiny of the world

After hearing Erda's predictions, Wotan tells Erda to return to her eternal slumber. He now realizes that the demise of the Gods is inevitable, but he has faith that greater and nobler spirits will emerge. Erda closes her eyes, slowly descends, and then disappears.

As the storm ceases, the moon rises. Siegfried lost the guidance of the forest bird and climbs blindly and impatiently toward Brünnhilde's rock. The Wanderer, a complete stranger to young Siegfried, interrupts his path and inquires where he goes. Siegfried advises the stranger that a bird was directing him to a flame-encircled rock where he must awaken a sleeping maiden. The stranger tells him that woodbirds sometimes chatter senselessly, and asks him how he learned to understand their singing. Siegfried recounts his adventures at Neidhöhle; that he was brought there by the treacherous Dwarf Mime to kill a life-threatening Dragon, and that after he tasted its blood, he was able to understand the songs of birds.

The stranger asks him who forged his Sword. Siegfried proudly asserts the he himself forged it from splinters that even Mime, the mastersmith himself, was unable to forge. The stranger continues to ask who created the mighty steel from which the Sword's fragments came. Siegfried, now irritated by the stranger's indulgence, replies naively that he does not know.

The Wanderer laughs, annoying the young hero even more. Siegfried asks why the stranger delays him with his questions; if the stranger knows the way to the rock let him show it to him; if not he should be silent. As the Wanderer criticizes his disrespect, Siegfried's patience explodes: all his life elders have interfered, especially the murderous Dwarf who had to be killed; he warns the stranger to be careful or else he will share Mime's fate.

When Siegfried inquires why a large hat overhangs the stranger's face, he is told that it is the way the Wanderer goes against the wind. Siegfried notices that the stranger has one eye missing, and concludes that it was no doubt struck out by another whose path he tried to bar; Siegfried warns him to leave or he may lose the other eye.

Quietly and lovingly, the Wanderer reproaches the impetuous boy, telling that if he knew his identity he would not scoff at him. He reveals that he bore love for his family, but that in his anger punished it excessively; the boy should not provoke him and awaken his wrath again.

Siegfried impatiently orders the stranger to step aside and let him pass. The Wanderer explains that the bird that was guiding him fled in fear of its life after it saw the Wanderer, the lord of the ravens. He tells Siegfried that it was he who put the maiden to sleep on the fire-encircled rock; if the young hero can pierce the flames, he can awaken and make her his bride. The Wanderer tests Siegfried's fearlessness and determination. He points to the glow visible on the heights, and warns Siegfried to retreat unless he wishes to be consumed by fire.

Siegfried declares that he does not fear the fire, and that he cannot be dissuaded from going straight to his promised bride and friend. In a last effort to deter him, the Wanderer holds out his Spear to bar Siegfried's path, telling him that the Spear is hallowed, and that it is the sacred instrument that broke and shattered his father's Sword. Siegfried exclaims vengefully that he has finally found his father's ancient enemy. He raises his Sword, and with one blow shatters the Spear in two; thunder and a flash of lightning project from the Spear toward the rocky heights where the flames have become brighter. The fragments of the Spear fall at the Wanderer's feet, and with resignation he quietly retrieves them.

It is in this confrontation with Siegfried that Wotan played out his internal conflict, the ultimate realization that his power to shape external events has ceased: Siegfried's destruction of the divine Spear symbolizes the annulment of the Godhead's power over events. The Wanderer had sought to bar Siegfried's path with the Spear upon which the Laws of the old order were engraved, but when Siegfried shattered the Spear, the inherent power of the old order was abolished. Siegfried and Brünnhilde represent the hope for a new world-order to emerge. Siegfried himself will remain ignorant, but as Erda hinted, it will be Brünnhilde's omniscient wisdom that will influence events in such a way that the world will be redeemed from all its evil forces.

As the Wanderer departs, he commands young Siegfried to pursue his destiny. The Godhead can no longer restrain the young hero; the fate of the world now weaves toward its destiny without the intervention of the Gods.

Act III - Scene 2: Brünnhilde's rock

Siegfried notices the increasing brightness of the fire, and joyously sounds his hunting horn as he makes his way toward the rock where his promised friend and bride await him. Fearlessly, he plunges into the blazing fire. The flames diminish slowly, and the rosy light of dawn gradually appears.

Siegfried approaches slowly, and then pauses in wonder. At first he sees a horse, and then a sleeping warrior in armor. He raises the warrior's helmet and becomes startled when a great mass of hair falls down. After he cuts the binding armor, he bolts back and turns into a frenzy of fear and excitement. In his amazement and bewilderment, he exclaims that the sleeping warrior is a woman, the first he has ever seen: "That is no man!"

Love's confusion

Pulsating emotions begin to stir in him. He invokes his mother whom he had never seen, but for whose love he has yearned, and who in his mind represents the incarnate conception of woman. Siegfried questions those throbbing sensations, asking himself if those stirring sensibilities represent fear. He tries vainly to arouse the sleeping woman, but she does not respond. In a despairing attempt, he kneels before her and presses his lips to hers. His long kiss awakens the beautiful sleeping maiden.

Brünnhilde opens her eyes and embraces life by solemnly raising her arms to greet the sun, earth, and sky.

Greeting to the World

Brünnhilde inquires who this hero is who has braved the flames and awakened her? She learns that he is Siegfried. The Valkyrie suddenly recalls her parting cry to Sieglinde when she announced the birth of the world's future hero: "Let him take his name from me; Siegfried, joyful in victory." Brünnhilde erupts into ecstatic rapture, realizing that her rescuer is none other than the fearless Volsung hero who is now fulfilling Wotan's prophesies. Siegfried and Brünnhilde bless Sieglinde, the mother who gave birth to him.

"O Heil der Mutter die mich gebar!"

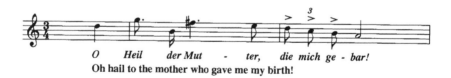

O   Heil   der Mut - ter,   die mich ge - bar!
Oh hail to the mother who gave me my birth!

Brünnhilde praises Siegfried as the most exalted of heroes, the man she loved even before he was born.

Rapture of Love

Brünnhilde and Siegfried then surrender themselves to their love, the blissful contemplation of the glory of their shared souls. Suddenly, Brünnhilde becomes fearful, realizing that she is no longer a Valkyrie maiden, but rather, a vulnerable mortal woman. When Siegfried tries to embrace her, she repels him, frightened and conflicted. In Valhalla she was an untouched, sacred virginal Goddess, but now that she has lost her Godhood, she is prey to mortal emotions that burn within her: yearnings that she is powerless to subdue or control. Fearful and sensing shame and disgrace, Brünnhilde asks Siegfried to torment her no longer, to leave her in peace.

Peace

Siegfried vows that their love invokes a new day that has dawned for both of them. Slowly, Brünnhilde's fears and protests dissolve as she yields to Siegfried's love. She praises Siegfried as the "noblest hero, wealth of the world, life of the life of things, laughter and joy; the star that shines above Brünnhilde, and the light of all living and loving."

Both embrace ardently and become transformed by the ecstasy of each other's love. In their happiness, they invoke their love: a love that illuminates and laughs at death.

Love's Resolution

The Valkyrie warrior, now transformed into a mortal woman, has discovered the nobility of love, humanity's greatest aspiration. Through Brünnhilde's all-consuming love, Siegfried will become empowered by wisdom, a force that will serve to foster a new world order of noble moral conscience that will redeem it from all of its evils.

Twilight of the Gods

("Götterdämmerung")

Music drama with a Prologue and Three acts

Music composed by Richard Wagner

Drama written by Richard Wagner

Premiere: Bayreuth Festspielhaus, 1876

Twilight of the Gods is the fourth and final music drama of
The Ring of the Nibelung ("Der Ring des Nibelungen")

Principal Characters in Twilight of the Gods

Brünnhilde,
  daughter of Wotan and Erda   Soprano

Siegfried,
  son of Siegmund and Sieglinde   Tenor

Gunther, King of the Gibichungs   Baritone

Hagen, son of Alberich,
  Gunther's half-brother   Bass-baritone

Gutrune, Gunther's sister   Soprano

Waltraute,
  a Valkyrie sister of Brünnhilde   Mezzo-soprano

Alberich, a smith,
  a Nibelung Dwarf   Baritone

Norns, daughters of Erda
  First Norn   Alto
  Second Norn   Mezzo-soprano
  Third Norn   Soprano

Rhinemaidens:
  Woglinde   Soprano
  Wellgunde   Mezzo-soprano
  Flosshilde   Contralto

Gunther's vassals and women of the Gibichung castle

Synopsis and Overview of Twilight of the Gods

At the conclusion of *Siegfried,* Brünnhilde and Siegfried consummated their holy marriage. As *Twilight of the Gods* unfolds, Brünnhilde sends her hero off for new adventures. Before departing, Siegfried gives Brünnhilde the treasured Ring as a token of his love; in exchange, Brünnhilde gives Siegfried her heroic steed, Grane.

In the meantime, Alberich sired a son, Hagen, with the Gibichung Queen, Grimhilde. Hagen, like his father Alberich, is consumed by his monomania to recapture the Ring for the Nibelungs and use its power to master the world.

In *Twilight of the Gods*, Hagen launches an insidious plot to capture the Ring. He tricks the unwitting Siegfried to drink a magic potion that obliterates his memory and induces amnesia; under its spell Siegfried, transformed by the Tarnhelm as the Gibichung King Gunther abducts Brünnhilde for Gunther, and secures the Ring from Brünnhilde. After Siegfried marries Gunther's sister, Gutrune, Brünnhilde realizes that she has been betrayed and swears revenge. She joins Hagen and Gunther in a conspiracy to kill Siegfried.

Hagen murders Siegfried. Brünnhilde forgives Siegfried after she learns that he was the victim of Hagen's deceit. She orders a funeral pyre erected for him and torches the pyre. Then she takes the Ring from Siegfried's finger, mounts her steed Grane, and rides into the flames to die with her beloved Siegfried.

The Rhine rises and the Rhinemaidens seize the Ring from Brünnhilde's ashes; the Ring has now returned to the Rhine and has become purified of Alberich's Curse. The blazing fires of the funeral pyre engulf Valhalla and destroy the Gods and their fortress. The cataclysmic doom of the Gods suggests that a new world order will emerge, a world of noble conscience and lofty human values.

Story Narrative with Music Highlight Examples

Prologue: Brünnhilde's rock

It is night. The fire surrounding Brünnhilde's rock gleams in the valley below while Siegfried and Brünnhilde sleep in their cave. Three veiled Norns, daughters of Erda, Goddess of wisdom, weave their mother's dreams into a mysterious golden rope that prophesies the destiny of the world. They unwind the rope, fasten one end to a branch of a tree, and the other to a projecting rock. As they weave, they recall the treachery of the Gods, the cause for their imminent downfall.

The first Norn relates that long ago Wotan came to the holy Well of Wisdom at the foot of the great World Ash-Tree, drank from the Well, and left an eye as tribute. Wotan then transgressed nature by breaking a branch from the tree, and molded it into a mighty Spear upon which he inscribed the Laws of mankind. The wound from the broken branch not only afflicted the tree, but the water also disappeared from the Well, rendering the tree leafless.

The second Norn relates that a bold young hero shattered Wotan's Spear that signaled the end of the God's power. In agonizing despair and resignation, the God summoned Valhalla's heroes to hew the remaining branches from the World Ash-Tree and place them around Valhalla.

The third Norn relates that the Giants built the great fortress of Valhalla for Wotan and his hallowed heroes. Now the fractured branches of the World Ash-Tree surround the mighty citadel, and when they are ignited, Valhalla will be destroyed by the flames; the Gods will fall and the world will descend into darkness.

Fall of the Gods

The first Norn cites the fires glowing in the valley below. She recalls that when Loge ran free he ravenously fed fires, but that Wotan has now subdued the cunning demigod. When Loge tried to free himself from Wotan by gnawing at the inscribed Laws on Wotan's Spear, the Godhead pierced his breast with the Spear, and then hurled him into the pile of the World-Ash-Tree's branches that encircled Valhalla.

The dark night confounds the Norns' vision; they complain that they can no longer feel the strands of their rope, unaware that the rope has been broken by the jagged rock. The Norns become terrified, believing that the broken rope is an omen signifying the end of their wisdom. As they disappear into the earth, they predict the imminent fall of the Gods, a consequence of the Gods' unconscionable evil acts.

As the sun rises, Siegfried emerges from the cave in full armor, now transformed from youthful adolescence into a man of heroic stature.

The mature Siegfried

Brünnhilde transformed by love

Heroic Love

Brünnhilde sends Siegfried into the world to perform fresh deeds of glory and achieve great fame. The former Valkyrie, transformed by the power of love, has conveyed all the wisdom she learned from the Gods to her beloved hero. She implores Siegfried that wherever he travels, or whatever deeds he achieves, he must never forsake his loving Brünnhilde, the woman who has devoted her heart and soul to him. Siegfried vows to honor their sacred oaths: as a token of his love for Brünnhilde, he gives her the Ring; she in return presents him with Grane, her steed that can no longer fly through the air, but will endure even fire for its new master.

The lovers exalt in their glorious union. They embrace in a last farewell, and then Siegfried leads Grane down the mountain to venture forth into the world.

Siegfried's Freedom

Brünnhilde remains on her rock. She gazes fondly and gestures rapturously at Siegfried as he departs on his Rhine Journey.

Act I – Scene 1: the Hall of the Gibichung castle

The great Gibichung castle is situated on a height above the Rhine. Gunther, the King of this fierce and warlike tribe, sits on his throne with his sister Gutrune at his side. Before them is their cunning half-brother, Hagen, the son of Alberich and their mother, Grimhilde.

Hagen

Gunther, who is indecisive and cowardly, asks Hagen how the Gibichung name is regarded on the Rhine. Hagen, secretly envious, hails his half-brother's renowned reputation, and affirms that their mother, Queen Grimhilde, indeed foretold his glory. Gunther resents Hagen for his superior wisdom, but he is disingenuously blind to Hagen's self-serving motivations, Hagen's obsession and secret vow to recapture the Ring for his Nibelung father, Alberich.

To pursue his objectives, Hagen unveils a malicious intrigue to entrap Siegfried. He expresses regret that both Gunther and Gutrune are unwed, and incites Gunther to wed the noble Brünnhilde, who dwells on a fire-encircled rock. But Hagen deliberately conceals his knowledge that Brünnhilde is already wed to Siegfried.

Hagen explains that Gunther could not penetrate the fierce fires surrounding Brünnhilde, but that Siegfried, the brave Volsung hero, could achieve it for him; he earned enduring fame by slaying the Dragon that guarded the Nibelung treasures. Hagen enlightens Gunther about the powers of the Ring: "The man who could wield its power could make himself lord of the world: Siegfried has won it."

Hagen announces that at this very moment Siegfried voyages down the Rhine, and that his arrival at the Gibichung Hall is imminent. He convinces Gunther that Siegfried would be indebted to Gunther if he promised him Gutrune's hand in marriage; in gratitude, the hero would bring him Brünnhilde and the treasured Ring.

Gutrune

Gutrune expresses her insecurity, wondering what charm she could possess for such a noble hero. But Hagen dismisses her doubts, assuring her that the hero will become enamored with her at first sight. Hagen assures her that after one taste of his magic potion the hero's memory will fade and he will think only of Gutrune. Before departing, Gutrune sighs, yearning for the moment when she will meet Siegfried.

As Hagen and Gunther speak, a distant horn call resounds, and knowingly, Hagen announces that the hero, Siegfried, who roams the earth in quest of great deeds, will soon arrive at the Gibichung Hall.

Hagen views the Rhine and notices a man and horse in a boat; the boat seems to be moving effortlessly upstream. He calls out to the hero and guides his boat to a mooring. With feigned sincerity and cordiality, Hagen welcomes Siegfried to the Gibichung Hall.

Gunther introduces himself as the Gibichung King. Siegfried, in the tradition of the ancient rituals, offers Gunther the choice of combat or friendship: "Let him fight me or be my friend!" Immediately, Gunther warmly welcomes Siegfried as his friend. Siegfried however, becomes somewhat bewildered that Hagen knew his name; the sinister Hagen explains that he recognized the hero by his strength.

With unabashed courtesy, Gunther offers Siegfried the freedom of the Gibichung castle. Siegfried reciprocates by offering his Sword, but Hagen slyly suggests that Siegfried offer the Nibelung Hoard instead. Candidly, Siegfried reveals that the treasure remains under the protection of the dead Dragon; however, he did seize the Tarnhelm, although he knows nothing of its value. Hagen immediately informs him that the metalwork is an ingenious Nibelung invention that can transform him at will, or enable him to fly to far off lands. Curiously inquiring, Hagen asks Siegfried if he took anything else from the treasures, prompting Siegfried to reveal that he seized the golden Ring, but that he gave it to the noble woman he loves. Hagen mutters resentfully, "Brünnhilde!"

Gutrune returns. She is a woman possessing no evil, but merely a gentle creature caught unwittingly in Hagen's web of evil purposes.

Hagen signals Gutrune to offer Siegfried the drinking-horn containing the magic potion. As Siegfried drinks he salutes Brünnhilde. Suddenly, Siegfried becomes the victim of the potion; he forgets Brünnhilde, compliments Gutrune, and then expresses his passionate love for her. Overwhelmed, Gutrune bows humbly and expresses her unworthiness for so great a hero. With faltering steps, Gutrune leaves the hall. Siegfried's eyes follow her as if he is bewitched.

Siegfried inquires whether Gunther has a wife. The King replies that he yearns for Brünnhilde, but he is unable to win her because he cannot penetrate the flames surrounding her rock. The mention of Brünnhilde fails to arouse Siegfried's memory, although he seems to be struggling to capture vague and forgotten thoughts. But the mention of fire arouses the hero; he offers to win Brünnhilde for Gunther, and in return requests Gutrune's hand as his reward.

Hagen now reveals his insidious plot. He advises Siegfried to invoke the Tarnhelm's magic and pierce the flames disguised as Gunther: after he seizes Brünnhilde he will spend the night with her in her cave, but she must remain inviolate. The next day he will lead her to the real Gunther and disappear; because of the Tarnhelm's magic power, the Valkyrie will never know that she has been deceived.

Siegfried and Gunther swear an oath of blood brotherhood, confirming that they agree to Hagen's plan. Hagen fills a drinking-horn with wine, and Siegfried and Gunther each slash their arms, allowing their blood to flow into the horn: "Happy and free I swear fidelity to my friend. Let our bond of blood-brotherhood bloom! If a brother breaks the bond, or becomes a false friend, the drops that we have drunk today, shall flow in streams, until the traitor atones!"

Oath of Blood brotherhood

Blü - henden Le - bens   la - bendes Blut   träufelt' ich in den Trank.
Life's freshened blood, I drop it here in the draught.

Siegfried offers the horn to Hagen, who violently slashes it with his sword, roguishly explaining that he took no part in the oath because his impure and ignoble blood would poison the drink. Siegfried affixes his armor and summons Gunther to follow him to his boat. Hagen is left to guard the hall during their absence. Gutrune, learning that they have gone in quest of Brünnhilde, erupts into an innocently joyful cry that anticipates her victory, "Siegfried! Mine!"

As the shadows of evening begin to fall, Hagen somberly begins his vigil, waiting patiently for his insidious intrigue to be fulfilled. Hagen gloats that Siegfried will return with the glorious bride, but more importantly, that he will return with the treasured Ring, Hagen's cherished prize with which he will enslave the world under Nibelung power.

Act I – Scene 2: Brünnhilde's rock

It is early evening. On the rocky height, Brünnhilde sits peacefully in front of her cave. She is overcome by happy memories as she thoughtfully contemplates and admiringly caresses Siegfried's Ring.

For the first time since Wotan laid her in slumber, she hears the rumble of thunder and the wild cries of a Valkyrie galloping through the air. It is her sister, Waltraute. Brünnhilde greets her joyously, hoping that she brings news that Wotan has forgiven her. Nevertheless, Brünnhilde bears no remorse; her punishment has brought her the love of the noblest of heroes.

Waltraute is agitated and anxious. She has sought Brünnhilde of her own free will, a rebellious act for which she has risked her father's punishment. Waltraute details the reasons she has sought her sister. Without Brünnhilde, Wotan no longer assigns his Valkyries to the battlefield. As the Wanderer, he roamed restlessly through the world, but he has now returned to Valhalla. He called all the Gods and heroes to a council to witness his inner torture, while he sat silently and dejectedly held the fragments of his Spear that were shattered by the young hero's Sword.

In despair, Wotan sent warriors to hew the World-Ash-Tree and ordered its branches placed around Valhalla, threatening to ignite them and destroy Valhalla and the Gods. But he has sent forth his raven messengers, Reason and Memory, and has promised that if they should return with good news, he would forget his grief.

Waltraute reveals that Wotan's thoughts are constantly preoccupied with Brünnhilde, and that he sadly recalls his farewell to her and the last kiss he pressed on her eyes. However, although the Godhead knows that his power has been crushed by the young hero, Brünnhilde remains his last hope to redeem the world by returning the Ring to the Rhinemaidens, thereby purifying it of Alberich's Curse. Waltraute has come to Brünnhilde to plead with her to return the Ring to the Rhinemaidens so that the Gods will be saved.

Brünnhilde erupts angrily and adamantly: "Never!" For Brünnhilde, the Ring represents Siegfried's pledge of love, a symbol more important to her than the survival of the Gods. Brünnhilde will not renounce Siegfried's love and cede the Ring, even if her refusal means that Valhalla will crumble in ruins. Brünnhilde, unyielding and intransigent, orders Waltraute to return to the holy council of Gods and inform them that Brünnhilde lives only for Siegfried's love, and that she will never surrender the Ring.

Waltraute cries out in defeat: "Woe's me! Woe to you, sister! Woe to Valhalla!" As Waltraute rushes off in despair, Brünnhilde seats herself before the cave and again contemplates the golden Ring affectionately.

Evening has fallen. In the valley below, Brünnhilde sees the surrounding fires flaring up furiously to the very height of the mountain. She hears Siegfried's familiar horn call and springs up joyously to greet him. However, it is not Siegfried, but rather, a strange, unknown warrior; the flames rise fiercely about him, but recede as he slowly advances.

The stranger — Siegfried transformed by the Tarnhelm into Gunther — has penetrated the blazing fire; the Tarnhelm conceals his face, and only his eyes are visible. Brünnhilde recoils in terror before the sinister apparition, shrieking frantically that she has been betrayed.

After a long silence, the stranger announces that the fire could not frighten him, and that he has come to take Brünnhilde as his bride, by force if necessary. Terrified, Brünnhilde tries to unravel the mystery by questioning the stranger's identity: he replies, "I am a Gibichung. Gunther is my name, and you must follow me."

Brünnhilde erupts savagely, convinced that she is witnessing another manifestation of Wotan's punishment. In a frenzy of despair she holds out the Ring threateningly to protect herself, but its power is ineffective, and the stranger advances toward her fearlessly; he struggles with her, and then seizes the Ring from her finger. Shattered and defeated, Brünnhilde sinks pathetically into his arms. The stranger announces that she is now Gunther's bride, and with an imperious gesture, he bids that they enter her cave. Hopelessly weakened and despairing, Brünnhilde obeys.

Before entering the cave, the stranger lingers, and then raises the Tarnhelm momentarily to reveal that he is Siegfried. He draws his Sword, and in his natural voice invokes a solemn oath to safeguard the woman's honor for Gunther. "Now, Nothung, you shall witness that my pursuit was pure; keep me from Gunther's bride, so that I may keep my promise to my brother."

He then lowers the Tarnhelm and enters Brünnhilde's cave, the unwitting betrayer of his own bride.

Act II – in front of the Gibichung castle

It is night. Hagen remains somberly on the steps of the Gibichung Hall, vigilantly awaiting the return of Siegfried — and the Ring. The arch-villain will remain unceasing in his diabolical attempt to entangle Siegfried, Brünnhilde, Gunther, and Gutrune in his inescapable net of evil.

Apparently asleep, Hagen's arm surrounds his spear, and his shield rests by his side. As the moon suddenly pierces through the clouds, Alberich is seen crouching before his son. Softly, he inquires if Hagen is asleep? Hagen sadly comments that long ago he had forsaken rest and sleep.

Hagen's eyes open and he is motionless. Speaking as if in a trance, he asks what message his Nibelung father brings him? Alberich inquires if his son is indeed as bold as the mother who bore him? Hagen replies that his mother gave him a brave heart, but complains bitterly that he has become dissipated, pale, wan, prematurely aged, unhappy and joyless.

Eagerly, Alberich advises Hagen to hate those who are happy, for then he will appreciate his father's sorrow and anguish. He advises Hagen to be cunning, strong and bold, for their enemies are now more vulnerable, wounded by their own unconscionable evil. Alberich reveals that he no longer fears the ruthless Wotan because the Godhead awaits his downfall, horror-stricken by his defeat at the hands of Siegfried, his own Volsung hero. He admonishes Hagen that the Nibelungs must be united, relentless and undaunted in their rage and hatred so that they can cause the doom of the despicable Gods and master the world.

Murder

Alberich reminds Hagen of events affecting the Nibelung's recapture of the Ring and treasure; that the fearless Siegfried now possesses the Ring but is unaware of its value and power; that he has given the Ring to Brünnhilde as a token of his love; and that if she returns the Ring to the Rhinemaidens all of their efforts will have been in vain. Alberich admits that he himself was too weak and unable to slay the Dragon, but he sired Hagen, whom he nurtured with passions of hatred and vengeance so he could help him destroy the Gods and recover the powerful Ring. Alberich pleads with his son: "Win the Ring for me, and ruin Wotan and the Volsungs! Swear it to me, Hagen, my son!" Hagen replies, "Fear not! "The Gold will be ours! Siegfried shall be murdered."

As Alberich departs and gradually fades into the darkness and shadows, he repeats his appeal to Hagen: "Swear to me, Hagen, my son! Be true to me! Be true!" Hagen dutifully replies, "To myself I swear, be silent and have no care!" Alberich disappears completely. Hagen, still motionless, keeps his eyes fixed towards the Rhine.

As dawn approaches, Siegfried emerges from the banks of the Rhine, now transformed back to his own form. He greets Hagen, buoyantly announcing that he has succeeded in winning the bride for Gunther.

Siegfried calls for Gutrune, the prize for which he braved the fires. Gutrune joins him and enthusiastically praises the hero who successfully passed through the flames unscathed. Siegfried proudly tells her that his adventure succeeded just as Hagen predicted: with his Tarnhelm disguise the Valkyrie thought she had yielded to Gunther. Although they slept together in the cave, he assures Gutrune that his Sword Nothung separated them to protect the woman's honor, and that the bride was inviolate when he brought her to the waiting Gunther the next morning. Gutrune hails the hero, "Siegfried! Mightiest of men! I faint in fear of you!" Now that Siegfried's task has been fulfilled, Gutrune proclaims joyously, "Let us prepare for our wedding!"

Hagen observes that the boat bearing Gunther and Brünnhilde nears the shore. Gutrune urges everyone to greet the new bride, praying that she may join the Gibichungs in happiness and bliss. Hagen blows raucously on his horn, calling the Gibichung vassals to assemble to welcome the arrival of their ruler and his new Valkyrie wife. He orders sacrifices to be prepared to celebrate the forthcoming royal wedding: the slaughtering of great steers on Wotan's altar, a boar for Froh, a lusty goat for Donner, and sheep for

Fricka so that the Goddess may bless the marriage. The vassals fill their horns with mead and wine and praise Hagen, their bridal herald.

After the boat bearing Gunther and Brünnhilde arrives, Hagen takes Brünnhilde ceremoniously by the hand and presents her to the vassals. They clash their weapons against their shields, hailing Gunther and their new queen.

Brünnhilde's eyes remain fixed to the ground while Gunther presents her as his wife, the crowning glory of the Gibichung name. She does not speak or raise her eyes as the wedding procession of Siegfried and Gutrune approaches. But Gunther greets them and proclaims, "Two blessed pairs are here united: Brünnhilde and Gunther, Gutrune and Siegfried."

Gutrune and Siegfried! Upon hearing Siegfried's name, Brünnhilde begins to tremble uncontrollably. In astonishment, she sees her hero in the embrace of Gutrune and exclaims incredulously, "Siegfried here? Gutrune?" Siegfried explains: "Gunther's gentle sister was won by me as you were won by him." Brünnhilde staggers and then sinks toward the ground. Siegfried, who is nearest to her, supports her in his arms; she looks up at him in astonishment and mutters, "Siegfried does not know me!"

Suddenly Brünnhilde sees the golden Ring on Siegfried's finger, and the reality of deceit begins to dawn upon her. She erupts violently, exclaiming that it was just last night that Gunther tore the Ring from her hand. In her confusion, she wonders how the Ring was transported from Gunther to Siegfried.

Hagen recognizes a critical opportunity to compound his malicious intrigue, and urges the vassals to carefully heed Brünnhilde's vengeful declaration. Siegfried quietly contemplates the Ring and assures her that he did not receive the Ring from Gunther, and Gunther disclaims any knowledge of the Ring. In the ensuing silence, all remain perplexed and bewildered.

With conviction, Brünnhilde explodes into impassioned outrage, denouncing Siegfried as the treacherous thief who stole the Ring from her. Pointing accusingly at Siegfried, she proclaims, "Not Gunther, but Siegfried is my husband. He possessed me in the bonds of love! Where shall I seek vengeance?" All turn inquiringly to Siegfried, but he denies that any woman gave him the Ring, and swears that he won the Ring by slaying the Dragon at Neidhöhle.

The devious Hagen again intercedes, claiming that if it was indeed Gunther who wrested the Ring from Brünnhilde, then the Ring rightfully now belongs to Gunther. Hagen accuses Siegfried of treachery, because he acquired the Ring through cunning. All erupt into frenzied cries of "Betrayed! Shamefully betrayed. Deceit, vile beyond all vengeance!"

Brünnhilde invokes the Gods in supplication: "Teach me a vengeance that is too severe to be spoken! Stir me to wrath that may never be stilled! Break Brünnhilde's heart into pieces, so that this traitor may taste a bitter death!"

Gunther tries in vain to calm Brünnhilde, and implores Siegfried to defend himself against her accusations. The unwitting Siegfried swears that her tale is false. He reminds Gunther that he swore blood brotherhood with him, and swears that he remained true to his oath; his Sword Nothung had lain between him and Brünnhilde. Enraged, Brünnhilde swears that Siegfried lies, vowing that on the bridal night the Sword indeed remained in its sheath, but its owner forced her into love.

Brünnhilde's revelation becomes explosive: Gunther immediately accuses Siegfried of betraying him; Gutrune implores Siegfried to swear that Brünnhilde speaks falsehoods; and the vassals demand that Siegfried uphold his word with an oath. Siegfried agrees, and the vassals surround him. Hagen raises his spear upon which Siegfried is to make his solemn oath. Siegfried places two fingers of his right hand on the spear-point, and solemnly swears that he spoke the truth: "Brünnhilde's story is false." He further vows that if he betrayed his brother, then Gunther may take this very spear and strike him dead.

Siegfried's Oath

SIEGFRIED

Hel - le Wehr,   hei - li - ge Waf - fe!
Shining spear! Hallowed weapon!

In a crazed and furious outburst, the humiliated Brünnhilde seizes Siegfried's spear and swears her own oath: "Shining spear! Hallowed weapon! May you bring Siegfried to his death, for he has broken all his vows!" Siegfried urges Gunther to restrain this wild woman who seems to be possessed by evil demons. He orders the celebrants to join the wedding feast, embraces Gutrune, and leads her into the hall.

Only Brünnhilde, Hagen, and Gunther remain. Confounded and bewildered, Brünnhilde, speaking more to herself than to the others, somberly seeks an explanation for these mysterious acts, but her wisdom fails her and she feels only sorrow and shame. Hagen prods Brünnhilde, "Let me avenge you! If Siegfried has violated his oaths, he must die!" At first, Brünnhilde laughs at Hagen, knowing well that one glance from the strongest c heroes would destroy him. Nevertheless, Brünnhilde accedes to Hagen's villainy and agrees to participate in a conspiracy to destroy Siegfried: Brünnhilde's revenge for Siegfried's betrayal of her.

As the impatient conspirators plot Siegfried's death, Brünnhilde regrets that she provided Siegfried with all of her knowledge of battle. Suddenly she recalls that there is one place where the hero is vulnerable; she never placed her protective spell on his back because she knew he would never turn his back to an enemy. The diabolical Hagen seizes his opportunity and proclaims: "And there my sword will strike!"

Hagen encourages Gunther to rouse himself to action, but the cowardly King implores Hagen to act on his behalf, because he is stronger and more cunning. Brünnhilde taunts Gunther because he is weak and shrinks from participating in Siegfried's murder. But the devious Hagen sways Gunther's resolve, hinting that when Siegfried falls, Gunther will possess the Ring, and with it, power beyond his dreams. Duped by the villainous Hagen, Gunther finally agrees to participate in Siegfried's murder, although he loathes the thought that he must face Gutrune with her husband's blood on his hands.

At the mention of Gutrune's name, Brünnhilde once again erupts into a furious outburst of vengeance: "From depths of despair it dawns on me now: Gutrune is the spell that took my hero from my side. Woe to her!" The cynical Hagen admonishes

Gunther that if Siegfried's death will grieve their sister, she should not be told of their plot. Instead, when they return from the hunt tomorrow Gutrune will be told that the hero was slain by a boar. All agree: "So shall it be."

The trio of conspirators invoke their oath: Brünnhilde and Gunther call upon Wotan to bear witness and consecrate their oath of vengeance against the traitor Siegfried. Hagen proclaims, "So let him die, this fair hero; the Hoard and the Ring shall be mine. Alberich, my father, fallen prince! Guardian of darkness! Nibelung lord! Soon you shall summon the Nibelungs to again bow down before you, the lord of the Ring!"

Siegfried and the vassals summon the wedding guests with their horns. The innocent Gutrune beckons Brünnhilde to join them. At first Brünnhilde stares at her blankly, and then recoils. At a sign from Hagen, Gunther seizes her, and the wedding procession proceeds to its consummation.

Act III: a woods near the Rhine

The Gibichungs are hunting. Siegfried's horn calls resound and are echoed by horns from the Gibichungs.

The swimming Rhinemaidens, Woglinde, Wellgunde, and Flosshilde, rise to the surface of the water, expressing their sadness as they mourn their lost Gold.

Rhinemaidens

The resonating horns cause the Rhinemaidens to wonder if they are announcing the hero who will restore the Gold to the Rhine. Siegfried, accidentally separated from the Gibichung game-hunters while chasing a prey, approaches them. The Rhinemaidens greet him, and then tease and prod him to explain his misadventure. Siegfried answers genially, suggesting that they had lured the prey he was pursuing. The Rhinemaidens immediately request the golden Ring that gleams on his finger. Siegfried refuses, explaining that he won the Ring by slaying a dreadful Dragon, and that he would not part with his possession, adding spiritedly that if he lost the Ring he fears a scolding from his wife.

The Rhinemaidens tease him about his stinginess and fearfulness of his wife. He tells them they can deride him to their hearts content, but that he will never cede the Ring. They continue to cajole him, a man so fair, strong, and suitable for love. Then, they disappear in the waters. Their jeers have wounded Siegfried and he calls for them to return, holding the Ring aloft to lure them back. When they reappear they solemnly forecast disaster: "Beware! A Curse hangs upon the treasure. Unless you cast it into the Rhine, you will be slain, here and today!" The Rhinemaiden's threats, however, fail to frighten Siegfried.

The Rhinemaidens continue to urge Siegfried to return the Ring to the Rhine so that it will be purged of its Curse. They warn him that there is no escape from the Curse because the Norns have woven it into their rope of destiny. Boldly, Siegfried proclaims that he will cut the Norns' rope with his omnipotent Sword; he would consider ceding the Ring for love, but not under a threat to his life.

The Rhinemaidens despair over the mad young man who prides strength and wisdom, but is blind to his destiny: he refuses to surrender the Ring that will bring him death; he swore oaths that he did not heed; and in his ignorance, he spurned the glorious and omniscient Brünnhilde. They advise him to go to Brünnhilde immediately, for today she will fulfill the destiny of the Ring.

As the Rhinemaidens swim away, Siegfried contemplates them, joking that if he had not wed Gutrune he would have sought love from them.

In the distance, Siegfried hears the Gibichung's horn calls. He reunites with the hunters, and is hailed by Hagen, Gunther, and the vassals. Hagen orders rest and food. All of their game is piled in a heap, wineskins and drinking-horns are filled, and all relax and talk of adventure. Hagen asks Siegfried how he fared with his hunting after they had lost sight of him. Laughingly, Siegfried relates his poor luck; he failed to kill any game but met three young waterfowl, who sung to him from the Rhine, and warned him that he would be slain today. Gunther trembles at Siegfried's revelation, and stares gloomily at the sinister Hagen.

Siegfried announces that he is thirsty, and Hagen hands him a filled drinking-horn. Siegfried in turn offers Gunther a drinking-horn. Gunther looks at it thoughtfully and gloomily, prompting Siegfried to express tenderness and compassion for his unhappy blood brother. Siegfried pours Gunther's drink into his own and asks Hagen if perhaps the King grieves over Brünnhilde's insolent behavior. Hagen seizes an opportunity to advance his intrigue and urges Siegfried to enliven Gunther by relating tales of his wondrous past adventures.

Siegfried proceeds to describe his youth. He relates that he was raised by the parasitic Mime, forged Nothung, slew the Dragon, and learned that the Dragon's blood enabled him to understand the songs of birds. He reveals that he killed the treacherous Mime, and then seized the Tarnhelm and the Ring from the Dragon's cave.

As Siegfried pauses, Hagen refills his horn. After Hagen places an herb in Siegfried's drink, he explains that it will serve to revive the hero's memories of the past. Siegfried looks thoughtfully into the horn, drinks slowly, and becomes stimulated to resume his story. He relates how a woodbird sung to him about the bride awaiting him on a fire-encircled mountain, and how he climbed the rock, conquered the fire, and found the sleeping Brünnhilde, whom he awakened with a kiss and then took for his bride.

At the mention of Brünnhilde, Gunther rises in astonishment, while the vassals remain mute and horrified. Wotan's two raven messengers, Reason and Memory, suddenly emerge from a bush, circle above Siegfried, and then disappear toward the Rhine. Hagen asks if Siegfried can understand the ravens. As Siegfried springs to his feet and gazes after them in the distance, he exposes his back to Hagen. Hagen seizes the opportunity and plunges his spear into Siegfried's back, and then shouts: "The birds have decreed your death!"

Siegfried swings his shield aloft to assault his murderer, but his strength fails him. The shield drops and he crashes upon it. Gunther and the vassals become horrified and ask Hagen why he slew Siegfried. Hagen replies, "Vengeance for a false oath!" Hagen turns away and slowly disappears while Gunther and the vassals, grief-stricken, sympathetic, and emotional, stand before the fallen hero.

Siegfried is raised to a sitting position by two of the vassals. His memory has fully returned. Instinctively, Siegfried hails his beloved wife, recalling the ecstatic moment of her awakening from her fire-encircled sleep: "Brünnhilde, holiest bride!" Siegfried's mind then begins to darken; he sinks back, and expires. Gunther commands the sorrow-stricken vassals to raise Siegfried's body and carry it in a solemn procession over the rocky heights to the Hall of the Gibichungs.

The moon breaks through the clouds, for a moment illuminating the mourners.

Funeral music

In the Hall of the Gibichungs, Gutrune emerges from her chamber, explaining that in her dreams she heard the neighing of Siegfried's horse and Brünnhilde's laughter. She thought she heard Siegfried's horn, and then became terrified when she dreamed that she saw Brünnhilde walking toward the Rhine. Gutrune rushes to an inner room to call to Brünnhilde, but it is empty. As she sighs and longs for Siegfried's presence, she sees the glow of torches in the distance. When she hears Hagen's rasping voice, she stands petrified with fear.

Hagen bids that all awaken, for he brings home a fine prize from the hunt. He greets Gutrune boisterously and cynically: "Up, Gutrune, to greet your Siegfried! The mighty has come home again." When Gutrune replies that she did not hear Siegfried's horn, the savage Hagen announces Siegfried's death: "His bloodless mouth will blow it no more; he will no longer hunt or fight, nor woo engaging women to love him."

Gibichung vassals arrive in confusion and agitation, followed by Gunther, and a procession bearing Siegfried's bier, which is placed in the center of the hall. Hagen gloats to Gutrune, "Your lover has been slain by the energy of a wild boar." Shrieking in agony, Gutrune falls on Siegfried's body while Gunther tries to comfort her. When she recovers, she repels her brother ferociously, accusing him of treacherously murdering her husband. Gunther replies by pointing to Hagen: "Not I, but Hagen was the accursed boar who dealt the hero his death."

Hagen steps forward defiantly: "Yes, I slew Siegfried! The traitor swore falsely on my spear, and as my prize, I claim his Ring!" Hagen and Gunther quarrel. As Gunther insists on claiming the Ring, Hagen becomes more assertive: "The Nibelung dowry is for the Nibelung's son." Hagen assaults Gunther with a savage fury. After they fight desperately, Hagen strikes him dead. Hagen then turns to the fallen Siegfried and tries to grasp his hand to seize the Ring, but he recoils in horror when the dead hero's arm raises itself threateningly against him. Gutrune and the vassals retreat in terror.

Brünnhilde solemnly appears at the threshold of the hall. She strides in slowly, and sternly bids that they cease their anguish. She announces that the betrayed Brünnhilde has returned for her due vengeance, because she has now learned the truth. She urges everyone to join her to lament the death of the noblest of heroes.

Gutrune cries out to her passionately: "Brünnhilde! Black with envy! You have brought misfortune and ruin to all of us. Your tongue goaded the men against Siegfried: woe the day when you came here!" Brünnhilde reveals that Gutrune was not Siegfried's true wife, but only a trivial love: "He had sworn his vows to me before he ever saw you." The gentle Gutrune, who unwittingly helped to weave Hagen's diabolical net, immediately transforms from love to hate and curses the dead Siegfried: "Ah, sorrow! I see the truth now! Brünnhilde was his true love whom he forgot through the drink!" Grieving and shamed, Gutrune turns away from Siegfried and mourns over Gunther's body. Hagen stands defiantly apart from the others, leaning on his spear and shield, and sunk in somber reflection.

Brünnhilde gazes at Siegfried's body. She turns to sorrow as memories of her beloved hero overcome her. She learned about Hagen's treachery from the Rhinemaidens, but unfortunately it was too late. Now she knows that Siegfried was innocent of any broken oaths.

Brünnhilde commands the vassals to pile up mighty logs for the hero's funeral pyre, and bring the steed Grane to be reunited with its master. Brünnhilde becomes transfigured as she passionately invokes a solemn tribute to the great hero, who committed treachery unwittingly. Yet, how did the truest of men become deceived? Brünnhilde answers her own question; she blames the Gods, denouncing Wotan for bringing misery upon Siegfried and Brünnhilde. She condemns the Gods: "Turn your eyes on my grief and distress, and on your own eternal guilt!"

Brünnhilde knew that Siegfried represented Wotan's holy purpose: through the hero's great deeds the Godhead hoped to escape the Curse that was consuming him. But unwittingly, the hero performed the Godhead's innermost Will by enlightening Brünnhilde to profound love, and she is now prepared to redeem the world from evil and purify the Ring of its Curse. As the ravens rustle about, Brünnhilde drives them off to Valhalla to bring Wotan the news he awaits; with great pity in her heart she murmurs: "Rest thou, rest thou, o God!"

Brünnhilde orders Siegfried's body raised on the pyre. She seizes the accursed Ring from his finger and gazes at it meditatively. She then solemnly addresses the Rhinemaidens: "I give you now what you have desired: you can win from my ashes all that you have wept for! The fire that burns me with Siegfried will cleanse the Ring of its Curse! The flood will wash the Curse away, and the ever-gleaming Gold that you unfortunately lost, will be pure again!"

Brünnhilde places the Ring on her finger, turns to the pyre, and takes a torch from one of the vassals. She addresses the ravens again: "Fly home ravens, and tell Wotan what you have heard here on the Rhine."

Brünnhilde hurls the torch into the pyre which erupts into bright flames. She turns to Grane, unbridles him, and lovingly asks the steed if he knows where they are traveling? As she points to the fire where Siegfried lies, Brünnhilde is overcome with rapture as she contemplates her holy reunion with Siegfried: "Oh but to embrace him, fall into his arms, and feel the maddening emotion to once more be his! Heiajaho! Grane! Let us greet our hero! Siegfried! Siegfried! See! Greet your wife!" Brünnhilde mounts Grane and rides triumphantly into the burning pyre.

Suddenly the fires die down. The Rhine swells vigorously and the three Rhinemaidens arise and seize the Ring from the ashes. Hagen becomes filled with terror and plunges madly into the Rhine in pursuit of the Ring. Woglinde and Wellgunde seize Hagen and drag him to his watery doom. As they swim away joyously, Flosshilde holds the recovered Ring exultantly aloft.

A red glow breaks through the clouds while the Rhine waters calm and gradually fall. The interior of Valhalla comes into view: Wotan sits gravely and silently among the Gods and heroes while holding his shattered Spear in his hand; with resignation, all of them await the end that had been foretold. The flames from Siegfried's funeral pyre then devour Valhalla and the Gods.

Redemption by Love

Flood and fire have redeemed the world by purifying the Ring from its evil Curse; a sense of hope remains that a new order of elevated conscience and noble ideals will replace humanity's inherent evil.

DICTIONARY OF OPERA AND MUSICAL TERMS

Accelerando - Play the music faster, but gradually.

Adagio - At a slow or gliding tempo, not as slow as largo, but not as fast as andante.

Agitato - Restless or agitated.

Allegro - At a brisk or lively tempo, faster than andante but not as fast as presto.

Andante - A moderately slow, easy-going tempo.

Appoggiatura - An extra or embellishing note preceding a main melodic note. Usually written as a note of smaller size, it shares the time value of the main note.

Arabesque - Flourishes or fancy patterns usually applying to vocal virtuosity.

Aria - A solo song usually structured in a formal pattern. Arias generally convey reflective and introspective thoughts rather than descriptive action.

Arietta - A shortened form of aria.

Arioso - A musical passage or composition having a mixture of free recitative and metrical song.

Arpeggio - Producing the tones of a chord in succession rather than simultaneously.

Atonal - Music that is not anchored in traditional musical tonality; it does not use the diatonic scale and has no keynote or tonal center.

Ballad opera - Eighteenth-century English opera consisting of spoken dialogue and music derived from popular ballad and folksong sources. The most famous is *The Beggar's Opera,* which is a satire of the Italian opera seria.

Bar - A vertical line across the stave that divides the music into measures.

Baritone - A male singing voice ranging between bass and tenor.

Baroque - A style of artistic expression prevalent in the 17th century that is marked by the use of complex forms, bold ornamentation, and florid decoration. The Baroque period extends from approximately 1600 to 1750 and includes the works of the original creators of modern opera, the Camerata, as well as the later works by Bach and Handel.

Bass - The lowest male voice, usually divided into categories such as:

> **Basso buffo** - A bass voice that specializes in comic roles: Dr. Bartolo in Rossini's *The Barber of Seville.*

> **Basso cantante** - A bass voice that demonstrates melodic singing quality: King Philip in Verdi's *Don Carlos.*

> **Basso profundo** - the deepest, most profound, or most dramatic of bass voices: Sarastro in Mozart's *The Magic Flute.*

Bel canto - Literally, "beautiful singing." It originated in Italian opera of the 17th and 18th centuries and stressed beautiful tones produced with ease, clarity, purity, and evenness, together with an agile vocal technique and virtuosity. Bel canto flourished in the first half of the 19th century in the works of Rossini, Bellini, and Donizetti.

Cabaletta - A lively, concluding portion of an aria or duet. The term is derived from the Italian word "cavallo," or horse: it metaphorically describes a horse galloping to the finish line.

Cadenza - A flourish or brilliant part of an aria (or concerto) commonly inserted just before a finale. It is usually performed without accompaniment.

Camerata - A gathering of Florentine writers and musicians between 1590 and 1600 who attempted to recreate what they believed was the ancient Greek theatrical synthesis of drama, music, and stage spectacle; their experimentation led to the creation of the early structural forms of modern opera.

Cantabile - An indication that the singer should sing sweetly.

Cantata - A choral piece generally containing Scriptural narrative texts: the *St. Matthew Passion* of Bach.

Cantilena - Literally, "little song." A lyrical melody meant to be played or sung "cantabile," or with sweetness and expression.

Canzone - A short, lyrical operatic song usually containing no narrative association with the drama but rather simply reflecting the character's state of mind: Cherubino's "Voi che sapete" in Mozart's *The Marriage of Figaro.*

Castrato - A young male singer who was surgically castrated to retain his treble voice.

Cavatina - A short aria popular in 18th and 19th century opera that usually heralded the entrance of a principal singer.

Classical Period - A period roughly between the Baroque and Romantic periods, the late 18th through the early 19th centuries. Stylistically, the music of the period stresses clarity, precision, and rigid structural forms.

Coda - A trailer added on by the composer after the music's natural conclusion. The coda serves as a formal closing to the piece.

Coloratura - Literally, "colored": it refers to a soprano singing in the bel canto tradition. It is a singing technique that requires great agility, virtuosity, embellishments and ornamentation: The Queen of the Night's aria, "Zum Leiden bin ich auserkoren," from Mozart's *The Magic Flute*.

Commedia dell'arte - A popular form of dramatic presentation originating in Renaissance Italy in which highly stylized characters were involved in comic plots involving mistaken identities and misunderstandings. Two of the standard characters were Harlequin and Colombine: The "play within a play" in Leoncavallo's *I Pagliacci*.

Comprimario - A singer who performs secondary character roles such as confidantes, servants, and messengers.

Continuo, Basso continuo - A bass part (as for a keyboard or stringed instrument) that was used especially in baroque ensemble music; it consists of an independent succession of bass notes that indicate the required chords and their appropriate harmonies. Also called *figured bass, thoroughbass*.

Contralto - The lowest female voice, derived from "contra" against, and "alto" voice; a voice between the tenor and mezzo-soprano.

Countertenor - A high male voice generally singing within the female high soprano ranges.

Counterpoint - The combination of two or more independent melodies into a single harmonic texture in which each retains its linear character. The most sophisticated form of counterpoint is the fugue form, in which from two to six melodies can be used; the voices are combined, each providing a variation on the basic theme but each retaining its relation to the whole.

Crescendo - A gradual increase in the volume of a musical passage.

Da capo - Literally, "from the top"; repeat. Early 17th-century da capo arias were in the form of A B A, with the second A section repeating the first, but with ornamentation.

Deus ex machina - Literally "god out of a machine." A dramatic technique in which a person or thing appears or is introduced suddenly and unexpectedly; it provides a contrived solution to an apparently insoluble dramatic difficulty.

Diatonic - A major or minor musical scale that comprises intervals of five whole steps and two half steps.

Diminuendo - Gradually becoming softer; the opposite of crescendo.

Dissonance - A mingling of discordant sounds that do not harmonize within the diatonic scale.

Diva - Literally, "goddess"; generally the term refers to a leading female opera star who either possesses, or pretends to possess, great rank.

Dominant - The fifth tone of the diatonic scale; in the key of C, the dominant is G.

Dramatic soprano or tenor - A voice that is powerful, possesses endurance, and is generally projected in a declamatory style.

Dramma giocoso - Literally, "amusing (or humorous) drama." An opera whose story combines both serious and comic elements: Mozart's *Don Giovanni.*

Falsetto - A lighter or "false" voice; an artificially-produced high singing voice that extends above the range of the full voice.

Fioritura - It., "flowering"; a flowering ornamentation or embellishment of the vocal line within an aria.

Forte, fortissimo - Forte (*f*) means loud; mezzo forte (*mf*) is fairly loud; fortissimo (*ff*) is even louder; additional *fff*'s indicate greater degrees of loudness.

Glissando - Literally, "gliding." A rapid sliding up or down the scale.

Grand opera - An opera in which there is no spoken dialogue and the entire text is set to music, frequently treating serious and tragic subjects. Grand opera flourished in France in the 19th century (Meyerbeer); the genre is epic in scale and combines spectacle, large choruses, scenery, and huge orchestras.

Heldentenor - A tenor with a powerful dramatic voice who possesses brilliant top notes and vocal stamina. Heldentenors are well suited to heroic (Wagnerian) roles: Lauritz Melchior in Wagner's *Tristan und Isolde.*

Imbroglio - Literally, "intrigue"; an operatic scene portraying chaos and confusion, with appropriate diverse melodies and rhythms.

Largo or larghetto - Largo indicates a very slow tempo, broad and with dignity. Larghetto is at a slightly faster tempo than largo.

Legato - Literally, "tied" or "bound"; successive tones that are connected smoothly. The opposite of legato is staccato (short and plucked tones.)

Leitmotif - Literally, "leading motive." A musical fragment characterizing a person, thing, feeling, or idea that provides associations when it recurs.

Libretto - Literally, "little book"; the text of an opera.

Lied - A German song; the plural is "lieder." Originally, a German art song of the late 18th century.

Lyric - A voice that is light and delicate.

Maestro - From the Italian "master"; a term of respect to conductors, composers, directors, and great musicians.

Melodrama - Words spoken over music. Melodrama appears in Beethoven's *Fidelio* and flourished during the late 19th century in the operas of Massenet (*Manon* and *Werther*).

Mezza voce - Literally, "medium voice"; singing with medium or half volume. It is sometimes intended as a vocal means to intensify emotion.

Mezzo-soprano - A woman's voice with a range between soprano and contralto.

Obbligato - An accompaniment to a solo or principal melody that is usually played by an important, single instrument.

Octave - A musical interval embracing eight diatonic degrees; from C to C is an octave.

Opera - Literally, "work"; a dramatic or comic play in which music is the primary vehicle that conveys its story.

Opera buffa - Italian comic opera that flourished during the bel canto era. Highlighting the opera buffa genre were buffo characters who were usually basses singing patter songs: Dr. Bartolo in Rossini's *The Barber of Seville*; Dr. Dulcamara in Donizetti's *The Elixir of Love.*

Opéra comique - A French opera characterized by spoken dialogue interspersed between the musical numbers, as opposed to grand opera in which there is no spoken dialogue. Opéra comique subjects can be either comic or tragic.

Operetta, or light opera - Operas that contain comic elements and generally a light romantic plot: Strauss's *Die Fledermaus*, Offenbach's *La Périchole*, and Lehar's *The Merry Widow.* In operettas, there is usually much spoken dialogue, dancing, practical jokes, and mistaken identities.

Oratorio - A lengthy choral work, usually of a religious nature and consisting chiefly of recitatives, arias, and choruses, but performed without action or scenery: Handel's *Messiah.*

Ornamentation - Extra embellishing notes—appoggiaturas, trills, roulades, or cadenzas—that enhance a melodic line.

Overture - The orchestral introduction to a musical dramatic work that sometimes incorporates musical themes within the work. Overtures are instrumental pieces that are generally performed independently of their respective operas in concert.

Parlando - Literally, "speaking"; the imitation of speech while singing, or singing that is almost speaking over the music. Parlando sections are usually short and have minimal orchestral accompaniment.

Patter song - A song with words that are rapidly and quickly delivered. Figaro's "Largo al factotum" in Rossini's *The Barber of Seville* is a patter song.

Pentatonic - A five-note scale. Pentatonic music is most prevalent in Far Eastern countries.

Piano - A performance indication for soft volume.

Pitch - The property of a musical tone that is determined by the frequency of the waves producing it.

Pizzicato - An indication that notes are to be played by plucking the strings instead of stroking the string with the bow.

Polyphony - Literally, "many voices." A style of musical composition in which two or more independent melodies are juxtaposed; counterpoint.

Polytonal - Several tonal schemes used simultaneously.

Portamento - A continuous gliding movement from one tone to another through all the intervening pitches.

Prelude - An orchestral introduction to an act or a whole opera that precedes the opening scene.

Presto, prestissimo - Vigorous, and with the utmost speed.

Prima donna - Literally, "first lady." The female star or principal singer in an opera cast or opera company.

Prologue - A piece sung before the curtain goes up on the opera proper: Tonio's Prologue in Leoncavallo's *I Pagliacci.*

Quaver - An eighth note.

Range - The span of tonal pitch of a particular voice: soprano, mezzo-soprano, contralto, tenor, baritone, and bass.

Recitative - A formal device used to advance the plot. It is usually sung in a rhythmically free vocal style that imitates the natural inflections of speech; it conveys the dialogue and narrative in operas and oratorios. *Secco*, or dry, recitative is accompanied by harpsichord and sometimes with other continuo instruments; *accompagnato* indicates that the recitative is accompanied by the orchestra.

Ritornello - A refrain, or short recurrent instrumental passage between elements of a vocal composition.

Romanza - A solo song that is usually sentimental; it is shorter and less complex than an aria and rarely deals with terror, rage, or anger.

Romantic Period - The Romantic period is usually considered to be between the early 19th and early 20th centuries. Romanticists found inspiration in nature and man. Von Weber's *Der Freischütz* and Beethoven's *Fidelio* (1805) are considered the first German Romantic operas; many of Verdi's operas as well as the early operas of Wagner are also considered Romantic operas.

Roulade - A florid, embellished melody sung to one syllable.

Rubato - An expressive technique, literally meaning "robbed"; it is a fluctuation of tempo within a musical phrase, often against a rhythmically steady accompaniment.

Secco - "Dry"; the type of accompaniment for recitative played by the harpsichord and sometimes continuo instruments.

Semitone - A half step, the smallest distance between two notes. In the key of C, the half steps are from E to F and from B to C.

Serial music - Music based on a series of tones in a chosen pattern without regard for traditional tonality.

Sforzando - Sudden loudness and force; it must stand out from the texture and be emphasized by an accent.

Singspiel - Literally, "song drama." Early German style of opera employing spoken dialogue between songs: Mozart's *The Magic Flute.*

Soprano - The highest range of the female voice ranging from lyric (light and graceful quality) to dramatic (fuller and heavier in tone).

Sotto voce - Literally, "below the voice"; sung softly between a whisper and a quiet conversational tone.

Soubrette - A soprano who sings supporting roles in comic opera: Adele in Strauss's *Die Fledermaus*; Despina in Mozart's *Così fan tutte.*

Spinto - From the Italian "spingere" (to push); a singer with lyric vocal qualities who "pushes" the voice to achieve heavier dramatic qualities.

Sprechstimme - Literally, "speaking voice." The singer half sings a note and half speaks; the declamation sounds like speaking but the duration of pitch makes it seem almost like singing.

Staccato - Short, clipped, detached, rapid articulation; the opposite of legato.

Stretto - Literally, "narrow." A concluding passage performed in a quick tempo to create a musical climax.

Strophe - Strophe is a rhythmic system of repeating lines. A musical setting of a strophic text is characterized by the repetition of the same music for all strophes.

Syncopation - A shifting of the beat forward or back from its usual place in the bar; a temporary displacement of the regular metrical accent in music caused typically by stressing the weak beat.

Supernumerary - A "super"; a performer with a non-singing and non-speaking role: "Spear-carrier."

Symphonic poem - A large orchestral work in one continuous movement, usually narrative or descriptive in character: Franz Liszt's *Les Preludes*; Richard Strauss's *Don Juan, Till Eulenspiegel,* and *Ein Heldenleben.*

Tempo - The speed at which music is performed.

Tenor - The highest natural male voice.

Tessitura - The usual range of a voice part.

Tonality - The organization of all the tones and harmonies of a piece of music in relation to a tonic (the first tone of its scale).

Tone poem - An orchestral piece with a program.

Tonic - The principal tone of the key in which a piece is written. C is the tonic of C major.

Trill - Two adjacent notes rapidly and repeatedly alternated.

Tutti - All together.

Twelve-tone - The twelve chromatic tones of the octave placed in a chosen fixed order and constituting, with some permitted permutations and derivations, the melodic and harmonic material of a serial musical piece. Each note of the chromatic scale is used as part of the melody before any other note is repeated.

Verismo - Literally "truth"; the artistic use of contemporary everyday material in preference to the heroic or legendary in opera. A movement particularly in Italian opera during the late 19th and early 20th centuries: Mascagni's *Cavalleria rusticana*.

Vibrato - A "vibration"; a slightly tremulous effect imparted to vocal or instrumental tone to enrich and intensify sound, and add warmth and expressiveness through slight and rapid variations in pitch.

Opera Journeys™ Mini Guide Series

Opera Journeys™ Libretto Series

Opera Classics Library™ Series

A History of Opera: Milestones and Metamorphoses

Puccini Companion: the Glorious Dozen

Mozart's da Ponte Operas

Fifty Timeless Opera Classics

PUCCINI COMPANION: THE GLORIOUS DOZEN

756-page Soft Cover volume

Each Puccini Chapter features:

COMPLETE LIBRETTO
Italian-English side-by-side

STORY NARRATIVE
with 100s of Music Highlight Examples

ANALYSIS AND COMMENTARY

Print or Ebook

A HISTORY of OPERA: MILESTONES and METAMORPHOSES

432 pages, soft cover / 21 chapters
featuring   **Over 250 music examples**
• A comprehensive survey of milestones in opera history
• All periods are analyzed in depth:
Baroque, Classical, Romantic, Bel Canto, Opera Buffa, German
Romanticism, Wagner and music drama, Verismo,
plus analyses of the "Tristan Chord," atonalism, minimalism...

Print or Ebook

OPERA JOURNEYS' COLLECTION: FIFTY TIMELESS OPERA CLASSICS

816-page Soft Cover volume

Print or EBook

*A collection of fifty·of the most popular operas
in the Opera Journeys Mini Guide Series,
each with Story Narrative and 100s of Music Examples,
PLUS insightful,in delpth commentary and analysis*

MOZART'S DA PONTE OPERAS:

Don Giovanni, The Marriage of Figaro, Così fan tutte

348-page Soft or Hard Cover Edition

Print or Ebook

**Mozart: Master of Musical Characterization;
Da Ponte: Ambassador of Italian Culture.**

*Featuring: Principal Characters, Brief Story Synopsis, Story Narrative, Music
Highlight Examples, and insightful in depth Commentary and Analysis, PLUS
a newly translated LIBRETTO of each opera
with Italian/English translation side-by-side.*

ORDER: Opera Journeys' Web Site www.operajourneys.com

OPERA JOURNEYS LIBRETTO SERIES
Print or Ebook

New translations (side-by-side) with Music Highlight Examples

•Aida •The Barber of Seville •La Bohème
•Carmen •Cavalleria Rusticana •La Cenerentola
•Così fan tutte •Don Carlo •Don Giovanni
•La Fanciulla del West •Gianni Schicchi
•Lucia di Lammermoor •Madama Butterfly
•The Magic Flute •Manon Lescaut
•The Marriage of Figaro •A Masked Ball
•Otello •I Pagliacci •Rigoletto •La Rondine
•Salome Samson and Delilah •Suor Angelica
•Il Tabarro •Tosca •La Traviata •Il Trovatore •Turandot

OPERA JOURNEYS MINI GUIDE SERIES

Print or Ebook

featuring 125 titles

- *Brief Story Synopsis*

- *Principal Characters*

- *Story Narrative*

- *Music Highlight Examples*

- *Commentary and Analysis*

•The Abduction from the Seraglio •Adriana Lecouvreur •L'Africaine •Aida •Andrea Chénier
•Anna Bolena •Ariadne auf Naxos •Armida •Attila •The Ballad of Baby Doe •The Barber of Seville
•Duke Bluebeard's Castle •La Bohème •Boris Godunov •Candide •Capriccio •Carmen
•Cavalleria Rusticana •Cendrillon •La Cenerentola •La Clemenza di Tito •Le Comte Ory
•Così fan tutte •The Crucible •La Damnation de Faust •The Death of Klinghoffer •Doctor Atomic
• Don Carlo • Don Giovanni •Don Pasquale •La Donna del Lago •The Elixir of Love •Elektra •Ernani
•Eugene Onegin •Falstaff •La Fanciulla del West •Faust •La Fille du Régiment
•Fidelio •Die Fledermaus •The Flying Dutchman •Die Frau ohne Schatten
•Der Freischütz •Gianni Schicchi •La Gioconda •Hamlet •Hansel and Gretel •Henry VIII
•Iolanta •L'Italiana in Algeri •Les Huguenots •Iphigénie en Tauride •Julius Caesar •Lakmé
•Lohengrin •Lucia di Lammermoor •Macbeth •Madama Butterfly •The Magic Flute
•The Makropolis Case •Manon •Manon Lescaut •Maria Stuarda •The Marriage of Figaro
•A Masked Ball •Die Meistersinger •The Mikado •Nabucco •Nixon in China •Norma
•Of Mice and Men •Orfeo ed Euridice •Otello •I Pagliacci •Parsifal •The Pearl Fishers
•Pelléas et Mélisande •Porgy and Bess •Prince Igor •I Puritani •The Queen of Spades
•The Rake's Progress •The Rape of Lucretia •The Rhinegold •Rigoletto •The Ring of the Nibelung
•Roberto Devereaux •Rodalinda •Roméo et Juliette •La Rondine •Der Rosenkavalier •Rusalka
•Salome •Samson and Delilah •Show Boat •Siegfried •Simon Boccanegra •La Sonnambula
•Suor Angelica •Susannah •Il Tabarro •The Tales of Hoffmann •Tannhäuser •Thaïs •Tosca
•La Traviata •Tristan and Isolde •Il Trittico •Les Troyens •Il Trovatore •Turandot
•Twilight of the Gods •The Valkyrie •Werther •West Side Story •Wozzeck

ORDER: Opera Journeys' Web Site www.operajourneys.com

Made in the USA
Columbia, SC
27 January 2021